SELF-PUBLISHING SECRETS 2019

UNLOCK THE STEPS TO PUBLISH YOUR BOOK

SHANNON BROWN

This book is a work of fiction. Names, characters, places, and incidents are the products of the author's imagination or are used fictitiously. Any resemblance to actual events, locales, or persons, living or dead, is coincidental.

All rights reserved. For information about permission to reproduce selections from this book, write to:

Sienna Bay Press

PO Box 158582

Nashville, TN 37215

www.shannonbrown.co

Copyright © 2019 Shannon L. Brown

Self-Publishing Secrets 2019/Shannon Brown—1st ed.

ISBN: 978-1-945527-19-7

LCCN: 2019901266

CONTENTS

	Who is Shannon Brown?	1
1.	Where do I start?	3
2.	What is self-publishing?	7
3.	What does self-publishing cost?	11
4.	Self-Publishing Glossary	14
5.	Do I need to pay someone to edit?	18
6.	Can't I self-edit?	22
7.	How do I find an editor?	29
8.	What is style?	34
9.	Ebooks, paperback, audiobook, hardcover?	36
10.	Do I need to buy an ISBN?	38
11.	Can I make my own book cover?	43
12.	Book Title	51
13.	Ebooks first. Usually.	54
14.	Should my ebooks only be on Amazon or everywhere?	60
15.	Should I upload my books myself or use an aggregator?	66
16.	How do I turn a Word doc into an ebook?	73
17.	How do I write the words on the back cover and the online sales copy?	77
18.	What are keywords?	82
19.	Should I set up a pre-order for my ebook?	86
20.	Do I want DRM?	91
21.	Do I need a publishing house name?	93
22.	How do I choose my book's price?	95
23.	Should my book be in print?	97
24.	Formatting a Print Book	104
25.	Do I need an LCCN?	113
26.	Do I have to buy a barcode?	116

27. How do I get my book into libraries and bookstores? 119
28. Should I turn my book into an audiobook? 128
29. Do I want a large print or hardcover version of my book? 135
30. Should I to pay to copyright my book? 137
31. This whole indie thing seems stressful! 139

Afterword 141

*To everyone who dreams of publishing books,
this is for you.*

And to my husband who has survived five years of a sometimes hectic life with an entrepreneurial wife. Thank you for encouraging my indie dreams. I love you!

WHO IS SHANNON BROWN?

I'm the author of nine books, several of which have become bestsellers. My fiction is under the name Shannon L. Brown, nonfiction as Shannon Brown.

I have published clean romance novels, mysteries for kids, and nonfiction. As of publication, I have a total of six novels and one novella, a journal, and this book. Other books will soon follow. That's the mark of a successful self-publishing career—the *next* book.

Before publishing fiction, I wrote hundreds of articles for newspapers and magazines. I have a degree in journalism/public communications with an emphasis in advertising and public relations. I also have a degree in secondary education. I only mention this so you'll know that I understand writing, marketing, and I love to teach. You'll get some of all three in this book.

As to my path to self-publishing, I tried to find a publisher for my books. I wrote my first novel in 1987. Yes, that long ago. I submitted it to a publisher and received positive feedback, but no contract. I wrote and submitted more books, but each was rejected. I once waited a full year for a very lovely rejection letter. In the middle of this, I searched for and found an agent who promised amazing things and did none of them.

My favorite of the books I'd written was a middle grade mystery for ages 8–12. I contacted many agents and editors about it, but publishers wanted a new type of book for kids, one no one had seen before. Kids and parents wanted an entertaining book.

The publishing industry changed. I could have beautiful covers made, hire the editors of my choice, and put out the book I wanted readers to have.

I released *The Feather Chase*, a modern-day Nancy Drew–type mystery, in 2014. That's now a three-book series. I also published a clean romance series set in Alaska, my home state.

When I started this journey five years ago, I didn't know how much I'd have to learn or how much the industry would change from that day to today. Through this process, I've been overwhelmed, I've burned out, I've healed and come back. My goal is to show you the best path for publishing your book, one that gives you a quality book you can sell but also leaves you happy and calm as much as possible. Let's not kid ourselves though. Self-publishing, like any profession, *is* work.

ONE
WHERE DO I START?

You're either writing a book or have completed one—or more—and are ready to publish. This may be your first book or your twentieth. You've either decided to self-publish or are checking out the possibility of self-publishing.

Before we go any further, I want to say that I plan to show you the path for publishing a *quality* book.

Quality publishing doesn't have to cost a fortune, but by having quality, your book can be shelved beside a book by a major publisher, and no one will be able to tell the difference. If that's your goal, you're in the right place!

You probably have many questions about self-publishing:

- *What do I do now?* Read the chapters in order and you'll know what to do.

- *Can I do this?* Absolutely.
- *Do I have the skills I need to do this?* Probably not yet, but you can learn them.
- *Is there technology involved? Will I have to learn new tech?* Yes and yes.
- *I heard about someone who wrote a book, put it on Amazon and made a bundle of money. I want that.* Probably not going to happen these days. Quality now rules.
- *I want to make lots of money, fast.* Self-published authors have the potential to make a great income, but that almost always takes multiple books and some marketing know-how. Get rich quick is possible, but most of us succeed over time.
- *Is self-publishing hard and complicated or easy and straightforward?* Both. *Self-Publishing Secrets* will give you the steps to have it feel straightforward. But you'll need to learn how to do something new and that can feel complicated at times.

All of these questions and more will be answered. If you take the process step-by-step, you'll take your stress level down a notch—or a hundred notches. It's easy to get overwhelmed. Remember when you learned to drive a car? You had to remember to keep your eyes on the road, use the turn signal, watch for pedestrians and other cars. But you did learn and now drive with ease.

Self-publishing a quality book can be done.

To help you, I have a Resources page on my website at shannonbrown.co/resources with links to helpful information. You'll see an (R) anytime you'll find more information there. This way, I can update as needed.

I'll also be updating the book every year. There were many changes in 2018 alone. Outdated information could be confusing and lead you in a wrong direction. It has become more and more important that self-publishing information be up-to-date.

Take time to search online to find self-publishing author groups. Facebook is usually best for this. They'll often have "indie" in their name, a synonym for self-published. You need a place to hang out and ask for recommendations, get marketing tips, and more. A local author group can help if they have a lot of indie authors.

Oh, and I have done my best to be accurate. If you knew me personally, you'd know I was super careful, did a lot of research, and *might* be a bit Type A. I can't be responsible for choices you make though and directions you go in publishing; they are your choices. As much as I've tried to be up-to-the-minute, you need to read the fine print before you sign up for anything.

I don't say much about marketing in this book because it's focused on the book itself and publishing it in the best way possible. Self-publishing has enough steps the first time. For more on marketing, follow my blog at shannonbrown.co.

First, let's take an important look at what self-publishing is and isn't. Then we'll get to step one.

Let's begin.

TWO
WHAT IS SELF-PUBLISHING?

In this chapter: Different publishing paths

Self-publishing is the process of taking your book from rough first draft to a finished, for-sale product. You are the publisher. There are many ways to publish a book though, and by looking at each, this concept will become clearer.

One bit of housekeeping here: I mentioned "indie" in last chapter. Most self-published authors now call themselves indie authors or even just an indie. The music and film industries started this years ago, and authors have picked it up. I'll use indie and self-published interchangeably throughout this book.

These are the forms of publishing

1. Indie: The most common method for self-publishing is when the author does every step herself or hires someone to do the pieces she can't do. (You don't want to see my attempts at book covers!) The author hires an editor, a book cover designer, etc. With this method, the author is similar to the contractor in charge of building a house who sub-contracts to an electrician and a plumber. This is what almost everyone I know does. The author retains all rights to the book and receives 100% of the profit.

2. Indie 2: You can also hire a company to manage the project for you. Instead of finding an editor, etc. yourself, you'd basically hand the manuscript over to them, and they would hand you back a finished book. This obviously costs more than the first method. You may also, depending on the company, lose some creative control. Ask about that. With a company like this, you still own all rights. The company is just managing each of the steps with the author involved in the process. The author retains all rights to the book and receives 100% of the profit.

3. Vanity Press: Another method is to use a company many refer to as a vanity press or vanity publisher. You give them money, often a lot of money, and they publish the book. The cost is high, the quality of the results can be less than equal to a traditionally published book, and you'll earn less. A vanity press usually makes its money up-front, not from book sales. Notice that editing is often extra. Please don't publish a book without editing! They may say they've "accepted" your book, making you feel like you've *finally* succeeded. Again, a vanity publisher isn't making the bulk of its money from the books it sells; it's from the packages sold. With some, you may still retain the rights, but because they've actually published your book, they take a significant cut of your profits for books, which are often priced high.

4. Small publisher: Sometimes a small publisher looks much like an indie publisher. They usually won't give you money up front—an advance on royalties. The book covers may be outstanding or not-so-great. They may have the book professionally edited or they may not. Anyone considering this path needs to research the company, what books they've published, the quality of the covers, and the editing. The book's rank on Amazon will reveal the sales volume, showing the marketing behind it. Be sure that the small publisher is able to do more than you would as an indie author. Some small presses are also sometimes asking an author to pay them money to publish the book, to share the expenses. The publisher owns the rights to your book for as long as your contract directs and will pay you royalties, a percentage of book sales.

5. Large publisher: This was—until recently—the main publishing method. A traditional, large, sometimes called legacy publisher will pay you an advance on future royalties—a check up front. You'll most likely need an agent to get a large publisher, and/or you'll need to meet someone from the publishing house at a conference. A large publisher will manage every aspect of the project. You probably won't have input into cover design, but some authors do. The publisher may or may not promote your book. The industry is changing every day it seems, and large publishers have cut back on book promotion, especially if you aren't one of the stars. The publisher owns the rights you've sold to them for as long as the contract directs and will pay you royalties—a percentage of book sales—after you have earned out (paid back through sales) the advance.

I'm going to assume that being an indie is what you want. Let's continue.

THREE
WHAT DOES SELF-PUBLISHING COST?

In this chapter: The major costs for a quality book

Most authors beginning their self-publishing journey have heard stories of someone who wrote a book and published it immediately with no editing and a homemade cover. That someone watched the money roll in.

Yes, that did happen. Young adult author Amanda Hocking did that. In 2010. In the past. *Past* is the important word here.

As the self-publishing industry has grown, reader's expectations have risen, probably because of competition. A book with an obviously homemade cover used to be okay. (Trust me, it's usually obvious when an author makes her own book cover.) Indie authors now have to meet the standards set by traditional publishers.

I hear story after story of authors who launched their book or even books then waited for sales. When they heard crickets, they began learning about self-publishing and discovered you rarely do well that way. After getting professional editing and covers, and learning to market, they do start to sell books.

You will need to spend money. This is a business and every business has expenses. It doesn't have to be thousands, but yes, some.

Two major expenses are editing and book cover design.

Upfront Costs

You can publish a book for less than $1,000 including professional editing and a book cover. My last romance cost about $850. The last of my children's books cost more because the cover is hand-illustrated by an artist, but even then I spent about $1,200. I could probably have done both for less—and many do—but, in the case of *The Chocolate Spy's* cover, I liked the artist and had used her on the previous book.

I could also spend a lot more and many do that too. Editing alone can cost thousands of dollars. A cover can cost that and more, but it doesn't have to. Indie authors have many choices.

You can also pay someone to format the interior of your book, taking it from a Word document to a publishable file. Many authors, but not all, do that themselves.

You can hire a publicist to market and promote your book. This is fairly expensive, and I only know of one author who did, but it did pay off for her financially.

My first book cost so much more than the next

books did. The cover and editing cost me about $4,000. It took a while to earn that back on a kid's book, but I eventually did.

There will be much more detail on all of this, but I wanted to dispel the myth that publishing a book is free. You can upload an ebook on Amazon and other platforms for free, but you need to attract readers who want to pay you for it. You'll need a well-edited book with a great cover to begin that process.

Action Step:

- **Think about how much you will spend to publish your book.**

FOUR
SELF-PUBLISHING GLOSSARY

Every industry has its share of words, phrases and slang you have to learn. Self-publishing is no exception. These are the most common terms you'll come across as you self-publish your book. Many of them will be covered in depth in later chapters.

Aggregators:

This is a company you can use like Draft2Digital or Smashwords. The author uploads his ebook file to the aggregator's site, and they submit it to the vendors you choose for sale. Aggregators also reach libraries and subscription services.

Barcode:

The code with the ISBN, and sometimes a price, on the back of a print book is a barcode.

BISAC:

You choose the Industry Standards and Communications (BISAC) code you for your book's category and that tells retailers the type of book it is.

Book Cover:

When the words "book cover" are used, it's often just the front cover of the book, the ebook cover. It can also be the whole print cover which includes the spine and back cover.

This is the legal rights to intellectual property such as books which give the copyright owner the ability to sell and distribute the work.

Distributor:

The author has an agreement with a distributor to get print books to booksellers. Ingram and Baker & Taylor are the major distributors in the US and in some other countries.

DRM:

Digital Rights Management (DRM) is a somewhat controversial method of securing your book against piracy.

EPUB:

A book must be formatted as an .epub for publishers other than Amazon.

Format:

Ebooks, paperback, hardcover, and audio are all book formats.

Formatting:

A book is formatted when it is taken from a manuscript, probably a Word document, and turned into what looks like a book.

Indie:

This is a shortened version of independent author and a synonym for self-published author.

ISBN (International Standard Book Number):

The 13-digit number you assign to your book. This is on your copyright page and on the barcode on the back of a print book, and identifies the format (print, ebook, audiobook, etc.) of your book.

Keywords:

A word or phrase that both describes your book and is searched for online. A book about having a home business might have keywords like "home office organization" or "home business ideas." These words are entered when you upload a book for sale and when advertising your book.

Metadata:

The specific details associated with your book that you enter when you upload it for sale is metadata. This includes the title, book description, format, price, publication date, and more.

Mobi:

Amazon uses the .mobi ebook format.

Offset Printing:

This is the traditional type of book printing. You order books; the printer you choose prints and delivers boxes of books to you. Then you store the books until they are sold.

Perfect Bound:

This is a standard paperback book.

Print:

This is a book printed on paper. If print is mentioned, it could mean paperback or hardcover, but would usually be paperback.

Print-On-Demand (POD):

The exact number of books needed are printed; none need to be kept in inventory. This might be one copy or hundreds.

Publisher:

You are the publisher of your book.

Returns:

When you publish your print books through IngramSpark, you can choose whether or not to accept returns. Unlike most retailers, bookstores historically have had the right to return books that haven't sold.

Spine:

The edge of the book between the front cover and back cover, best described as the side that faces out on a shelf.

Traditional Publisher or Trad:

A publisher of books such as Penguin or Simon & Schuster.

Trim Size:

This is the size of your print book. You format your book to this size, then it is printed on larger paper and trimmed to the selected size.

FIVE

DO I NEED TO PAY SOMEONE TO EDIT?

(The answer is yes, but we'll talk about some other things before we get further into money.)

In this chapter: Learn about the importance of editors

People are often confused about editing, believing that correcting grammar and putting commas in the right place equals an edited book. A book can have the correct commas but be unreadable. I've come upon those, and you may have too—a grammatically correct novel with massive plot holes, or nonfiction that feels rambling in places, but too brief or confusing in others. That's a poorly edited book.

Quality editing includes revising, rewriting, *and* those pesky commas.

First, the word "editor" can be confusing when you're new to self-publishing. In the traditional publishing world, you have an editor, and he or she is your main contact at the publishing house. That person may or may not edit—that is, make changes to—your book. In the self-publishing world, an editor is always a person you've paid to suggest changes to your book.

As indies, we have to duplicate parts of the traditional publishing process, so understanding that world is important. Note: Indies often use "trad" for traditional publishing.

We aren't trad, but trad is usually known for quality, so let's look at how they create a quality book.

Even if you're a John Grisham or J.K. Rowling, they will edit your book. Grisham's contact at the publishing house, the editor, either reads through his manuscript or has someone else do this developmental or content edit.

That editor will give detailed instructions on where to tighten the story, work on characters, enhance or change the setting, fix awkward sentences—the list goes on.

If the book was nonfiction, it might have a chapter or idea you need to flesh out, eliminate or clarify.

This edit turns a so-so book into one that achieves the book's goals: it's readable, entertaining (if that's a goal), clear and solid.

The book you've written may make perfect sense to you and your significant other because you both know what you *meant* to say, but it may not be clear to a new reader.

After you've made the recommended changes—optional or not, often depending on the publisher— the book goes to the line editor who makes sure everything flows well. He finds inconsistencies in fiction such as the fact that your main character's eyes were blue on page one and green on page 59, or you used the word "just" or "really" 500 times in the book. That's just tedious to your reader and really slows the book down. (See how easy it is to use those words?)

After you've made the changes, the manuscript goes to the copyeditor, and she spots micro issues with things like grammar and punctuation. Then there's a proofreader before it goes to print, someone who catches the errors everyone else missed.

As an indie author, you have to duplicate the end result. Whether or not you use multiple editors, you want to have a quality book. You're going to have to spend some money here. The book cover and editing are the two major expenses for indie authors.

There's that money thing again. You'd like to save money and not hire an editor.

You're so close to the story that it's difficult if not impossible for you to see the errors. You no longer see the small errors and sometimes the big problems too.

You can't skip editing. Even if you've had published books, articles, or even been working as a paid editor for years, editing yourself will be challenging. I've sold over 800 articles and published nine books, but I *know* I need a paid editor to have the best book.

An editor improves your writing. It becomes a challenge for a writer to edit her own work because she knows what she wanted to say, but she's seen it so many times that she can no longer see it clearly. An editor comes to the project with a fresh viewpoint.

You're still thinking that surely you and the English teacher you know can handle editing. No, please don't do that unless the English teacher (I hear this a lot) or secretary (also often heard) is used to editing for publication. It's unlikely that he or she has ever edited a long work like a book, understands what's expected and undesirable in your genre, and knows *Chicago Manual of Style*. (More on this later.) English majors, to my surprise, know scholarly editing conventions but not those used in the publishing world. Secretaries can turn out a quality letter but probably haven't been trained for publication either.

Knowing more about self-editing, the types of editing, and how to find an editor is important, so we'll dive into that in the next two chapters.

Action Step:

- **Keep Reading**

SIX
CAN'T I SELF-EDIT?

Yes, you can and should self-edit! This will greatly help the book, but you can't substitute self-editing for professional editing.

In this chapter: Many methods of self-editing

Saving Money

Before we get into paid editing, there are quite a few things you can do to both spend less on editing and have a higher quality book. Even if you have a trad book contract, these will apply. You want to deliver the highest quality book you can without stressing out so much that you can't sleep or try to bite your significant other's head off when he/she speaks to you.

It's time to find the pesky mistakes. How many times have you been reading a book and were getting into it when a misspelled word or other error stopped you in your tracks? Your writing may have punctuation and other errors. No matter how careful I am before formal editing, my projects always do. Let's fix those.

Cheap and free editing methods (combined with paid editing, not instead of it)

Fact Checking

Almost every book has something in it that the author has to research. I had to call the Idaho Department of Fish & Game (I lived in Idaho then) for my first book because I had a bat in it and I wanted to make sure it acted bat-like. (The series may be for kids, but it's accurate.) Every detail needs to be correct because readers will know the beach is five blocks from the town square, not ten as you said. A bad review mentioning inaccuracies in your book may appear on Amazon. Reviews will be mentioned a lot in this book, but they matter and impact sales both for good and not-so-good. Save yourself the stress and check every fact *before* publication.

These next self-editing techniques can strengthen your book and save money. Having a clean document means that your editor can see the remaining things that need to be fixed. She won't be correcting the basics and missing the big picture.

Set it Aside

Let your book rest before you edit. Setting your book aside for at least a week, two or more would be even better, clears it from your mind and allows you to see it with fresh eyes. You were so caught up in your own writing that you couldn't see the words clearly anymore. Now, it's as if someone else wrote it. You may be surprised about what you notice. Remember not to read it at all during the cooling-off period, or you'll undo the benefit.

When I read a rested book, some sections are awesome (Wow! I wrote that?!) and some confusing (Oops! I'd better fix that).

Read it

Slowly read your book. If it's in Word, changing from single to double-spacing can help with this. Printing it out instead of reading it online can also make a big difference for seeing it with fresh eyes. We seem to view things differently in different formats.

Listen to it

At some point in your editing process, read the book out loud or use one of the many text-to-speech apps to read it to you. I read mine out loud, but some authors prefer to have the book read to them. I wait until my book is near publication, but doing this at any point in the editing process would be helpful. If you stumble over a word, sentence or paragraph as the reader, or it sounds awkward, improve it. You'll be surprised at all the things that stand out. This process can make your book much better.

Alpha and Beta Readers

It's a great idea to have someone else read your writing. Anyone will do for this so your spouse, best friend, or Aunt Sally will be fine. One warning on this: people close to us often love everything we do. Remember when your mother praised your second-grade efforts? It can be a challenge to get them to see the details, so ask them to be honest. These are alpha readers—a term I've rarely seen but which fits. They're helpful people you trust who read your book before anyone else does. These readers see your book before it has been professionally edited.

Once your book is fully edited and, other than final proofreading, and ready to be published, beta readers can be important and can have multiple purposes. They're great first readers of your polished book. They can also be part of your marketing efforts by telling people how much they enjoyed your book through word-of-mouth marketing and reviews. Here we're talking about first readers. The English teacher or secretary you know is perfect here and can give useful input.

Some authors use beta readers brilliantly. They have a group of people who have volunteered to be the first to read their books and give feedback. Sometimes an ending or another element will be changed by the author because multiple beta readers didn't like it.

Honesty moment here: While I love the idea of beta readers, mine haven't given much useful input. They tell me they love the book. Thank you, but I was hoping for details about places that confused you or points you wish had been different. I need to sort this out myself, but if you do manage beta readers well, they're a very good thing.

Free and paid editing tools

This comes with a warning label: an app is software on a computer, and a computer isn't a human. Obvious, huh? This is important because computers don't always get grammar and punctuation right. Don't blindly accept every change. Consider each one. With that said, I also carefully consider every change when a human edits for me.

When the app's right, it saves you money and time.

Your first line of defense is the spell checker in the app where you wrote your book. Since editors usually want to work on your book in Word using Track Changes, move the book from the other writing app if you used one and put it into Word. Now run the Word spelling and grammar checker.

Next, consider at least the free version of one or more of the following apps. They'll scan for spelling, grammatical, and punctuation errors.

Grammarly:

Grammarly (R) is an app that leaves word processing grammar and spell-checkers in the dust. No matter how many times you've read your writing—even out loud—you've missed something, maybe many somethings. I recently thought I'd finished a project and put the text through Grammarly. It found errors, including the same word side by side—the the. Our amazing brains are so sophisticated that they do an autocorrect. We can read something and skim over errors because our mind fills in the gaps.

Grammarly finds many of those gaps. In addition to finding basic errors, the app will also show you when you've overused a word or chosen a word that's overused in general. You can test Grammarly with the free version.

Just as with Word's checker, it won't be right every time. (It's that whole computer, not human, thing.) The female main character in *Crazy About Alaska* is a real estate agent, and Grammarly wanted to put a comma between real and estate every time.

I run every project through Grammarly at least once, often at each step of the process. If it finds one typo right before I click "publish," it paid for itself.

I don't use Grammarly inside Word; I upload my text to their site. I haven't enjoyed having an app running and correcting me as I work. You may love it.

ProWriting Aid:

ProWriting Aid (R) is growing in popularity among writers. It has the perk of working well with Scrivener, a popular writing program. There is a free version, but it's only for up to 500 words, so irrelevant for authors. This app checks for issues including style, grammar, overused words, and passive voice. It also offers synonyms when you double- click on a word.

ProWriting Aid gives the option of clicking on Summary, Style, Grammar, Overused, Cliches, and more.

They are less expensive than Grammarly or Ginger. I found that they missed some errors that Grammarly found, but I love ProWriting Aid's suggestions for changes to passive voice and other places it thought could be improved.

Ginger:

Ginger(R) is another, similar app. You can try it first for free, but the free version offers a limited selection of the Premium tools. Using the free Chrome plugin, the app will edit everything you type online. They have other apps too. Ginger can also translate text into 40 languages, similar to the free Google Translate. (Please note that this type of translation won't be perfect and shouldn't be used for the published version of a book in another language. You need a native speaker or someone fluent in a language to be part of a book translation project.)

This app will offer suggestions for rephrasing in addition to spotting the usual errors.

Action Steps:

- **Set your book aside.**
- **Find beta readers.**
- **Test at least one editing app.**
- **Read your book out loud.**

SEVEN

HOW DO I FIND AN EDITOR?

In this chapter: Different types of editing and how to choose an editor

Finding your editor(s) is one of the most important things you'll do. When you have a good editor, he or she helps improve your book which makes your life happier and can increase your bottom line.

Good editing is an important difference between a professional-quality book and one that reads "self-published."

For fiction, I use a developmental editor, a combination line and copyeditor, and a proofreader.

You know from the "What does self-publishing cost?" chapter that self-publishing a quality book isn't free. I usually spend about $700 on editing per novel. Less on nonfiction because I have years of experience with it, but I still use an editor.

You hand your editor the best quality book you can;

they make changes and suggestions before sending it back to you.

These suggestions will probably be made in a Word doc. Even if you write in Scrivener (which I highly suggest), you will compile to Word and send that file to your editor. Your editor will make the corrections in Track Changes (an easy tool to use), and you will accept or reject each change. With that said, my developmental editor edits a paper printout, so the rule isn't 100%.

I don't accept all of my editor's suggestions, especially when she gives me an exact rewording. By pointing out a problem, she has let me know that I need to go back and fix it. I make a change that solves the problem and fits my book and style. When it comes to commas and other punctuation, I do as the expert says.

Knowing the types of editing will help you choose wisely.

Developmental, Substantive or Content Editing

An editor who uses any of these titles, will find confusing areas, places where you under or over explained.

In fiction that might be a chapter or scene that needs to be shifted to another place or deleted for clarity, pacing, or because it's unnecessary. Plot holes, consistency with characters, and setting are also reviewed.

In nonfiction, clarity is king. Chapters need to flow from one to the next. Some places may be under or over explained.

We've all read books that felt confusing or slow. A developmental editor helps fix that.

Copy or Line Editing

This editor comes on the scene when you've finished the other edits. She will check for run-on sentences, overused words, grammar, spelling, and more. I keep a list of words I routinely overuse and add to the list as I notice that a book is heavy in a particular word.

Some editors combine these first two types of editing into one package. They'll take care of both, a step at a time, and you'll edit in between. I prefer having two different pairs of eyes on my book, but you may thrive with the other process.

Proofreading

This won't be done until the last moment when your book is 100% complete. Any missed errors should be caught by this editor. She could be someone you know who is very good at spotting mistakes. Using more than one proofreader can be helpful too.

Finding your editor(s)

It's often best to find your subcontractors, people such as your editor and book cover designer, through suggestions from other authors. Ask in your author Facebook groups—and if you aren't in any author Facebook groups, find some today.

Check an editor's website. If you like what you see, contact them and look at how they work.

When my usual editor had to cancel once at the last minute, I found someone on UpWork (R), and she did a good job at a great price. She wasn't as skilled as my usual editor who has decades of experience, but good.

Some professional editors may be booked months in advance so don't delay.

Test Edit

When you find an editor or several editors that you believe would be good, ask each if they would do a sample edit on a few pages or a chapter if the chapter is short. Some won't offer this service, but others will. It may be free if they do, or there may be a charge.

My first paid editor was terrible and cost more than I've paid for any other editor. Many times more. She didn't have the vision for my story. She tried to change characters, didn't seem to understand that they were in a small town . . . it was weird.

I learned to have an editor do a sample edit of several pages so I can see her style. When you have several editors do that, you're also able to compare them to see the errors each picked up and to note the things they want changed that you believe are great as is. Always consider the change though because the editor may be right and you may be holding onto drivel. Or not.

An important note: You are responsible for the book(s) you publish. Yes, you're hiring an editor or editors, but the final version you upload is your responsibility. I have seen multiple times when errors have been found in a published book, and the authors say, "But I paid for an editor!"

Even the best editors can miss something.

As I read through the print proof (the sample copy an author orders before making the book live for publication) of *The Treasure Key*, I realized that the dad was in the car and then he wasn't. I found the error in time and fixed it, but it had been professionally edited, I'd read it multiple times, and my professor husband had read it. We'd all missed what now seems obvious.

You're the final authority on whether or not your book is well-edited and ready for publication. Read it one last time after everyone else is done before clicking submit. You may be tired of the project and ready to let it go, but you'll thank yourself later if you do catch an error.

Action Steps:

- **Decide the type(s) of editing you want.**
- **Search for editors.**
- **Hire an editor or editors.**

EIGHT
WHAT IS STYLE?

In this chapter: Giving your books the standard style of traditionally published books

In publishing, "style" is a reference tool that helps the publisher know the standards for grammar, punctuation and more.

Chicago Manual of Style (CMOS) (R) is the standard for book-length fiction and nonfiction that isn't scholarly. AP Style is the standard for newswriting.

Why does this matter? Style is the glue that makes professionally published books feel consistent, even if that's invisible to most readers.

For example, *Chicago Manual of Style* says that numbers are spelled out from zero through one hundred, with only a few exceptions. They also use the serial or Oxford comma; that's the comma before the "and" in a list.

Oxford comma example: Shannon enjoys strawberries, blueberries, and grapes.

There are exceptions to this rule, mainly if adding the comma in a more complex sentence than the one above results in ambiguity. It's helpful to check their book or use the online version which allows you to search more easily for what you need.

These details may seem silly (I know you're ready to skip to the next chapter), but it is an industry standard, gives your book consistency from beginning to end, and your books from one to another. It's an important professional step.

Publishers, and you're a publisher now, are also allowed to have a house style. That means that no matter what Chicago says to do, you can do it a different way. Sometimes Chicago's rules on hyphenation result in a confusing or not standard word. Placemat became place mat according to Chicago. I chose to go with the standard use in stores selling them —placemat. Use house style wisely. Don't go crazy with it.

Choose the correct edition of Chicago Manual of Style, currently the 17th. Subtle changes occur. The last update included changing from e-book to ebook, something many of us were happy to embrace.

I do my best to get style right. Then I hire editors who know Chicago and will fix everything I missed.

Action Step:

- **Look at the *Chicago Manual of Style* online (R), buy a 17th Edition print version (R), or get it at your library.**

NINE
EBOOKS, PAPERBACK, AUDIOBOOK, HARDCOVER?

In this chapter: Different formats of books and which ones you may want

When authors decide to self-publish, they tend to be in the ebook-only camp, or they have dreams of seeing their books everywhere.

Ebook, paperback, hardcover, and audiobook are each a "format," a way your book can be read or listened to. These formats will be discussed in depth in later chapters, but it's important to decide which ones you want for your book, both now and in the near future.

You need to have an ebook. Rare exceptions to this include books that must be on paper to be used such as a journal or coloring book. Sometimes a writer who isn't an ebook reader doesn't see the need for ebooks. Trust me on this; you'll sell ebooks.

You *need* to have a print book, generally meaning paperback, if you're publishing nonfiction or children's.

It's a good format to add in other fiction genres, but may not be as critical initially. You will sell print books no matter the genre, but it's a matter of volume.

Audiobooks become more important every day, taking a larger and larger share of the market. Seriously consider doing an audiobook at some point.

Hardcover is usually optional. Unless your field is heavily using hardcover, you'll probably want to save this for last, if ever.

Study books similar to yours, *successful* books, and see what formats they're in. And don't just look at the discounted books that hit the bestseller lists because of a sale; check out the available formats of the books that are on the lists for a while.

With this said, focus on what you can manage both with time and money. It's better to do one format well than to spread yourself so thin that quality suffers and stress ensues. One rule you should stick to though is to not choose print alone for fiction.

Action Step:

- **Decide which format(s) you want to start with.**

TEN

DO I NEED TO BUY AN ISBN?

In this chapter: What ISBNs are and whether or not you need one

An ISBN (International Standard Book Number) is a 13-digit number that is assigned to your book. An ISBN I assigned to *Falling for Alaska* is:

978-0-989438-4-3

This particular ISBN identifies not only this book but the paperback version of it. Wherever that version of the book is sold, whether an online site in the U.K. or a bookstore in Australia, it will have the same ISBN. Each section of the ISBN means something, but that isn't something you'll likely ever use. Example: 0 or 1 is for English.

The number is an identifier that's especially useful when working with bookstores and libraries. The ISBN is also part of the barcode on the back of a print book. You can search online booksellers using an ISBN, but I doubt customers do very often.

Every format of a book—paperback, hardcover, audiobook—needs its own ISBN. It isn't optional. Ebooks are different.

Ebooks

ISBNs are optional with Amazon's ebooks. Some authors use them and some don't. If you plan to be exclusive to Amazon, you may not need an ISBN for your ebook. Amazon assigns their own number, an ASIN (Amazon Standard Identification Number), to every ebook, those with and those without ISBNs.

With that said, many authors are exclusive to Amazon for awhile, then choose to sell through many vendors, then move back to Amazon, etc. Having an ISBN for ebooks, including on Amazon, means that the same number will stay attached to that book. If you do use an ISBN for ebooks, it won't show on the Kindle book page.

Some other book vendors will also have an identifier number of their own.

We'll get into this in more detail later, but there are two ways to sell ebooks. You can sell directly through a company such as Amazon or Apple Books, or you can upload your books to a third party known as an aggregator such as Draft2Digital or Smashwords, and they will upload the books to the seller. You can also combine the two methods.

Some of aggregators offer a free ISBN, or you can upload your own. Whenever you use a free ISBN, that number has been bought by that company and will show them as the publisher, just as it will show you as the publisher if you buy one yourself. You should still own the rights to the book. Smashwords requires an ISBN, but it can be a free one from them, to distribute your book to Apple or Kobo. If you choose to use a free ISBN, you can't take that number with you if you leave that company.

Overdrive, a major distributor of ebooks to libraries, also requires an ISBN, but that could be a free one from Draft2Digital or Smashwords.

Confused? Don't be. The basics are that you usually won't need to buy ISBN for an *ebook*, but that it can be helpful if you publish beyond Amazon.

I have always used an ISBN for ebooks because I didn't know I could do otherwise in the beginning. I would still choose to use one though because I know what the number is wherever that ebook is sold. There are successful authors who don't use ISBNs for ebooks, though.

Print

Your paperback or hardcover book will need an ISBN, either paid or free. A reader can use the ISBN to search for your book on Amazon, Barnes & Noble, the UK's Waterstones, and others.

The two main paperback book printers are Amazon and IngramSpark. We'll go into each deeply in the "Print" chapter.

Amazon offers a free ISBN. Before you accept their offer, you need to know that Amazon is the publisher of record, that your Amazon page will show "Independently published" as the publisher instead of your publishing name, and that the ISBN is only valid on their site. It can't be used if you also, either now or in the future, decide to publish with IngramSpark or any other print publisher. If that's okay with you, then you're set.

If you publish with IngramSpark, you will need to provide an ISBN.

Audiobooks

You may or may not need an ISBN for audiobooks. In general, you need an ISBN for every format and that would include audiobooks. Since this is a section of the industry that seems to be changing by the day, it's best to check with the service you choose to create and publish your audiobook to see what's needed.

Amazon's ACX will assign a free ASIN, just as with ebooks, but if you're non-exclusive with ACX, an ISBN would be needed. (Exclusive and non-exclusive are explained in the "Should I turn my book into an audiobook?" chapter.)

Findaway Voices allows up to two ISBNs, one for retail and one for libraries. If you're planning to sell a "small volume of books," they can provide a free ISBN. Since you probably aren't planning to sell a small volume of books, you should probably upload at least one ISBN to them.

Where to get ISBNs

In the US, you can only buy ISBNs from Bowker (R). In the UK, they're sold by Nielsen (R). ISBNs are free in some countries including Canada. Check Resources (R) for a link if you outside the US. As an American, I've only used Bowker.

Bowker Pricing:

Buying one ISBN is most expensive. The block of ten costs much less for each one and the price per ISBN drops significantly with the block of 100. Bowker often has sales, so keep checking the site. Remember that you need an ISBN for every format with the possible exception of ebooks, so if you plan to have more than one book and in more than one format, buying at least the block of ten makes sense. I started with that, used them up, and bought a block of 100 on sale.

Once you've published your book, return to the Bowker site and enter the book's details so it will be registered and discoverable by its ISBN. Just purchasing it doesn't make that happen.

The ISBN will be good forever for that format of the book, unless you make *significant* changes to the book's text, change the title or the size of the book. Simple changes and corrections not requiring a new ISBN include pricing, minor adjustments to text, or a new book printer.

Action steps:

- **In the US, decide about free vs. paid ISBN(s), often based on the vendors and printers you choose.**
- **If you need paid ISBNs, go to Bowker (R).**
- **Outside the US, check your country's ISBN terms (R).**

ELEVEN
CAN I MAKE MY OWN BOOK COVER?

In this chapter: Book cover options and details

It may be cliché, but books are judged by their covers. A good book deserves a good cover. Your book cover is the first thing a potential buyer sees. There are many, many stories of authors who made their own covers, sold few books, then paid for a professional cover, and their sales turned around.

Authors wanting to make their own covers usually fall into one of these camps:

I'm strapped for cash.

OR

I'm creative and want to express myself.

The days when a homemade book cover will do are long gone. Today, readers expect an indie book to have a cover equal to one on a traditionally published book.

Please don't make your own cover. This is especially important for fiction. There are a lot of books that have bad covers. Readers have millions of books to choose from on Amazon, so they probably won't click on the one with the poor cover.

Simply knowing Photoshop isn't enough. *If* you know Photoshop or InDesign, you may be able to make a nonfiction cover. If you want to make your own fiction covers, spend a couple of days going through books in the genre to see what's selling. When you've made a cover you think looks great, get honest feedback from people you trust.

I paid for the cover on this book because I know it matters, and even though I understand design and composition, I also know that cover design isn't my strong suit.

Choosing a cover designer is near the front of this book because they can be booked months in advance. Spend time on this decision now rather than waiting until you need the cover the following week.

Cover designers are artists even if they're assembling photos on the cover and not hand-illustrating. Just as Picasso is different from Rembrandt, one designer's covers will have a different style from another. They often specialize in a genre or genres. Yes, they have the tech skills to make any cover, but understanding what's currently selling in your genre can't be overstated. This *will* impact sales.

If you're publishing a business book, it has to look like other business books. Literary fiction has some flexibility, but covers on genre fiction—romance, thrillers, sci-fi, etc.—must fit the genre. Someone will scan through books on a site or in a store and not stop if it doesn't fit what they're expecting. Quality book covers offer clues to what's inside. Every romance reader knows that a man with his shirt off is on a steamy romance, not a sweet and clean romance.

Check the top 100 on Amazon in your genre and study the covers. You'll probably see a pattern. Your book has to look like those books. Don't try to break the rules as a new author. Save that for when you've sold a million books. You can be a trendsetter then.

Premade

Don't panic about the price of covers. Premade book covers are the intermediate step between doing it yourself and having a custom cover made. Many designers make covers and sell them on their site or on a site with other premade covers. These are often ebook covers (that's just the front cover) with an extra-fee option for paperback (with a spine and back cover).

Prices vary, but you can find great covers for less than $100, sometimes much less. Be careful though because some sites may include covers that look like a beginner may have made them. Do your market research so you know what you need and want.

If you're searching for a cover with images of people in the design, be open to changing your character's hair color and some other physical details. It can be hard to let go, but I've had to do that even with custom covers when I couldn't find a photo that looked like my character.

Most sites will only sell the cover once but check that in the details. This doesn't mean the photo or photos won't be used again, but that specific cover won't be sold again.

Also check to see if they'll do a print cover for IngramSpark if that's what you need. It has the extra step of being uploaded on a template and some don't want to make them.

Custom Covers

Finding your designer may be as easy as a Google search, but it's always a good idea to start with recommendations. An author sometimes notes the designer's name on the copyright page or in acknowledgments. The indie world is very helpful and welcoming, so you can ask indie authors you've met online who does their covers and they'll probably share the name. This book's cover designer did the cover for Tammi Labrecque's *Newsletter Ninja*. I liked it, contacted her, and she gave me his name.

Check out a designer's portfolio on her website. Remember that every graphic designer has a style. Make sure they've made covers in your genre and that those covers fit your vision. One designer and I started to work on a cover then realized that her style didn't fit my vision. We parted ways on good terms, and I found someone else through a fellow indie author.

There are sites where custom, inexpensive covers can be bought such as Fiverr, Freelancer, and UpWork. Read the designer's reviews before buying and carefully go through their sample covers.

I will suggest you find one who speaks a language you do. I bought an inexpensive cover for a giveaway from someone who spoke little English, and the back and forth about changes were challenging. That's not to say that you shouldn't work with a cover designer in another country. Half of my cover designers live outside the US.

Book covers, often determined by genre, may have photos, other graphic images, or be hand-illustrated or hand-lettered. A cover could be a combination of several of these.

You can provide the photos and other images for a book cover, but they're often included in the price. Always ask about photo rights. It's important that you have the commercial rights to use that image on a book cover. A professional designer knows that. Read the license agreement. Never (NEVER) use an image you've found online on a site other than one specializing in stock photos for projects like this. You don't want to be sued.

Tip: When I was learning about book covers, I found The Book Designer's site (R). The monthly ebook cover contest gives reviews of submitted covers and explains why they do or don't work. I advise you to go through a few months of these before you decide on a cover designer. You'll have a much better idea of what you're looking for, and if you'd been considering it, you'll also know if you have the skills to make a cover yourself.

Cost

An author could spend over $1,000 or less than $100 on a cover. Somewhere in between will probably give you want you want. My recent romance covers cost about $150. Remember that price doesn't necessarily equal quality, but it can.

If you need an illustrated cover—one where an artist draws an image for you—that will probably cost more than most covers with photos. Book covers for children's books, even ones in the 8-12 age range I write for, usually have illustrated covers. I spent well over $1,000 for my first illustrated cover. Then I found someone on 99 Designs who worked for about $500 each for books 2 and 3. On 99 Designs, the author sets a price for a cover, gives the details they want, and designers submit rough drafts of covers, which you choose from and develop.

The entire print cover can be almost completed but held until you know the exact page count, which gives the spine's thickness. Five hundred pages need a thicker book than 150 pages. You aren't required to give the designer the finished back cover text until that time either, but you will need to keep the space in mind. A highly decorated back cover can have less room for words.

Your designer will also need to know if you want ebook alone—less expensive—print, audiobook, or all three. An ebook cover is completed at the time of designing because it's basically just the front cover of the book. A print book has the front cover, a spine, and the back cover.

If you're starting with one or two formats, that's fine. Additional formats can be added later so don't stress about this too much. It's a good idea to ask your designer what the process and costs would be for doing those.

You can also add on bookmarks and social media headers, often for a small amount extra.

Cover Rights

Most designers will keep the rights to your cover; you're given the rights to use it in normal ways, online for sale, for marketing, etc. If you want to put your cover on commercial products such as t-shirts, make sure your rights from the designer allow that and/or negotiate that up front. Also, check the rights for that use for any images on the cover. Again, I'm not a lawyer.

If you use 99 Designs (R), you're given the full rights to your completed book cover. If you use an inexpensive site like Fiverr (R), read the rules for that designer to make sure you do own the copyright and for no extra money. Having the full rights is nice, but not standard in the industry.

Genre

Genre is so closely tied to a book's cover design that being clear about that is next. Every book must have a genre, the exact category where it fits with other similar books. You need to know your genre so you can place it in the right category on a site like Amazon and so your potential reader knows exactly what to expect when they choose your book. Meeting and exceeding a reader's expectations are keys for success.

Unless you're certain about your genre, go to Amazon and search for books you believe are in that genre. Read the blurbs. Were you right? If yes, scroll down to the book's categories and click on each to see the covers and your competition. If not, try other search terms until you do find books like yours.

A business book may fit into "business" but also "social media for business" and "home based." Science fiction could be niched down to "space exploration" or "alien invasion." What do the books in your genre have in common?

Action Steps:

- **Research competition.**
- **Search for and buy a pre-made cover or . . .**
- **Research and choose a cover designer, and order a custom cover.**

TWELVE
BOOK TITLE

In this chapter: Book title tips and methods for creating yours

Some authors know their title. It's easy. It came to them either before they wrote a word or during the writing or editing process.

Other authors, myself included, need to do more to find their best title.

If you fall into the first category and have a winning title in mind, do an online search with your proposed book title in quotation marks to see if anything odd appears. You probably don't want a major crime or something like that with the same name, even if you write books about crimes.

Next, go to Amazon and put the title in to see if there's another book with that title. You can't copyright a title so you could use the same title. Think about it first, though.

I'd had a title in mind for my first book for years. I called it that when I talked about the book. Then, when

I was ready to publish it, I checked and a fairly new, popular book for the same group of readers had my exact title. I chose a new title. I might not have done that if it was in a non-competing category.

If you need help with a title, browse through similar books to get a feel for the titles they're using. Is there a pattern? If so, seriously consider following that pattern. Are there keywords you should have on your cover, words that cue the reader in to the genre?

One of my personal favorite methods is to make a list of every word about my book that pops into my mind, without filtering them. I combine them randomly to see what I get. I use a thesaurus if I need more, similar word options. Titles I like start to form. Remember to check the title on Google and go to Amazon before running with your favorite.

When you have a title you love, you still have a bit more to do. If your book is nonfiction, you'll probably need a subtitle and, if you plan to have other, similar books, possibly a series name. If your book is fiction and part of a series, you'll need a series name and possibly a tag line for the book cover, something that intrigues potential readers. As always, check your competition to see how they're doing it.

The subtitle and series name will be shown on the Amazon page next to your book cover. You want a potential buyer to be clear about your book so they know if they should click on it. Choosing words someone may use when searching for books like yours can help.

Again, check your competition to see what they've used, then come up with some options. Check to make sure your idea fits the genre and works hard for your book.

As I write each of these, I find it's helpful to let it rest overnight, see how I feel about it the next day. New ideas often come to me when I step back from a project for a few hours or days.

Don't leave this to the last minute. Then this may be your scenario: your cover designer needs a name for the book cover! Make it up in a hurry! Wish you'd spent more time on it.

Work on it in advance, give it time, and you'll be happier.

Action Steps:

- **If you don't have a book title yet, create one.**
- **For nonfiction, create a subtitle and, if needed, a series name.**
- **For fiction, if needed, created a series name and tag line.**

THIRTEEN
EBOOKS FIRST. USUALLY.

In this chapter: Where ebooks are sold and in-depth details about each

Having a book as an ebook is important for almost all books. Many people prefer digital. This is good news for an author because it's instant gratification for the reader. They can click, buy, and read. It's pure profit for you because you don't have printing costs to deduct.

Ebooks should be one of the first formats you release unless you have a book which won't work well with ebooks such as one that's meant to be written in like a journal or coloring book.

You may have heard about or read stories online about ebook sales dropping. Actually, that isn't true. Ebooks published by trad publishers are tracked, and they all have ISBNs. A few years ago, trad raised their ebook prices to be closer to print prices. Their ebook sales dropped. Many indie ebooks are invisible to the system that's being used to track ebook sales. Many, many ebooks sell every day around the world.

Pricing is key. If your ebooks are priced too high—if you've used the trad publishers as your guide—then you may be pricing yourself out of the ebook market. Research similar books to see what they're charging. As I mentioned before (sorry if it's becoming repetitive), look for books that are selling well but aren't just high in the ranks because of a short-term price reduction.

Major Retail Ebook Stores

These are the major sellers of English-language ebooks roughly in sales order. But some authors will sell a high volume of books on Kobo or GooglePlay, so this is variable.

Amazon's Kindle Direct Publishing (KDP)

Apple Books

Kobo

Barnes & Noble Press

GooglePlay

There are other sellers, either small enough that they're unimportant at this time, or in languages other than English.

It's easy to upload to the various companies either directly or through a third party, an aggregator (see the next chapter).

The royalty, the amount the author receives from the book's selling price, is fairly consistent among companies.

Each vendor (or aggregator) will require a method for paying you, usually made as a deposit to your bank or PayPal, but this varies by company and sometimes your country.

You can simply upload to every vendor and be done with this chapter. You don't have to make a bunch of decisions. If you do want more information, keep reading. Even if you upload to every company, and you probably will if you aren't exclusive to Amazon, it can help to see what makes each different.

As a way to decide which vendors to focus on, the perks of each, and how to benefit from using that vendor, let's get into the details of the top ebook sellers. There will be more about ebooks in the next two chapters and in the pre-order chapter.

Amazon's Kindle Direct Publishing (KDP)

Books can be read on a Kindle device or with the app on almost any device.

Easy to upload the files to.

70% royalty if prices set between $2.99-9.99, 30% royalty on lower or higher prices, with a delivery fee.

Setting a price to free is at Amazon's discretion.

Payment is 60 days after the end of the month of the sale. A July 15 sale would be paid at the end of September.

KDP Select is an optional program which has a chapter devoted to it.

Apple Books (2018 name change from iBooks)

Books can be read on an Apple device.

Easy to upload the files to directly—if you use a Mac. If not, you'll need to go through an aggregator.

70% royalties on sales no matter the price with no delivery fees.

There isn't an upper cap on pricing for royalties, but you probably don't want a single ebook priced over $9.99.

Ability to set price to free.

Payment is 30-45 days from the last day of the month. A July 15 sale would be paid before or about September 15.

A book file can be prepared in iBooks Author which uses a variety of templates (with options for interactive books), with Pages, or uploaded as an .epub that's been created elsewhere.

Promo Codes—Authors can request up to 250 codes per book which are valid for four weeks from the request date. Give the coupons to reviewers, bloggers or other media for a free copy of your book.

If you upload a new version of the book, previous purchasers will be notified and told of the changes.

Kobo Writing Life (Rakuten Kobo)

Kobo may not be familiar to many in the US, but they are a major player reaching an international market of over 200 countries. Their books can be read on a Kobo ereader or with an app on other devices. Kobo partnered with Walmart in 2018, so ebooks listed with them are also on Walmart's site.

Easy to upload to their Kobo Writing Life author platform or Kobo can be accessed through an aggregator.

70% royalties for books $2.99 USD and over. 45% for

books under $2.99 USD. Prices need to be 20% less than the physical edition of the book if there is one. (To check rules for other currencies, click on My Account and Terms of Service.)

Ability to set price to free.

Ability to set a different price for each of fifteen countries.

Paid within 45 days after the end of the month—if you meet the $50 minimum threshold. A July 15 sale would be paid about September 30.

The online platform doesn't currently track pre-order sales or returns.

Promotions tab—Available upon request. Clicking on this tab shows free and paid promotion opportunities on the Kobo platform, a perk of going direct to Kobo that isn't available otherwise.

Kobo Writing Life has a blog and podcast.

Barnes & Noble Press (changed from Nook Press in 2018)

Some are saying Barnes & Noble's sales are decent right now. When they stopped selling internationally several years ago, sales dropped for many, but perhaps they'll grow.

Only sells ebooks in the US.

Read on a Nook device or with the app on other devices.

65% royalties for $2.99 and above, 40% for below $2.99. No delivery fee.

Ability to set price to free.

Barnes & Noble Press recently introduced a paid advertising platform.

Google Play Books

Books can be read on any Android or iOS device.

Books may be more discoverable on Google searches.

The other vendors are fairly straightforward to work with. Create an account, upload a book, set the price, click publish. GooglePlay has some quirks.

First is the access to Google Play. New authors fill out a form (R), submit it and are notified by email when they're accepted. It's on a limited basis, but everyone I know who's recently applied has gotten in.

Google Play is the one site that routinely drops the price of your ebook from the price you've set. While this sounds fine, it can wreak havoc with your Amazon books because Amazon wants to have the lowest price. When Amazon matches the new lowest price, this can cut into your profits. It's often suggested that you set your GooglePlay price higher to compensate for the upcoming drop.

Royalties are 52% and based on the price you set, not the lower price the book may have sold for.

Acton Step:

- **Decide if your book needs to be an ebook.**

FOURTEEN

SHOULD MY EBOOKS ONLY BE ON AMAZON OR EVERYWHERE?

In this chapter: Whether or not you want your ebooks to be exclusive to Amazon

Note: this is *only* about ebooks. Print and audiobooks have different rules which will be discussed in later chapters.

KDP stands for Kindle Direct Publishing. If you publish an ebook with Amazon—99.99% of indies do—you will be publishing to KDP.

The question about KDP Select vs. wide may be the most asked question about self-publishing, both for first-timers and pros.

KDP Select is a 100% optional choice when uploading an ebook to Amazon KDP. You'll have to ask yourself if you *only* want to sell that ebook on Amazon.

"Wide" is the commonly used term for offering your ebooks for sale with multiple vendors which include Apple Books, Barnes & Noble Press, Kobo, and GooglePlay.

One very important note here: in order to use KDP Select, you need to upload your ebooks directly to Amazon, not through Draft2Digital, IngramSpark or another third-party company. There are more opportunities with Amazon when you're direct to them.

If you're new to this discussion, you may be asking yourself why an author would only want to sell ebooks with one company.

There are clear benefits to both wide and Select. With Select, keep in mind that you're only signing up for a 90-day period.* This isn't a permanent, irrevocable choice beyond that commitment. The amount of money earned from a full-priced book purchase remains the same whether or not the book is in Select.

Let's look at the pros and cons.

KDP Select's Benefits

Note: Only one of the following two promotions is allowed during the 90-day period, not a free one and one at a reduced price.

Benefit 1: An ebook priced between $2.99 and $9.99 usually receives 70% of the sales price. A $4.99 ebook would receive about $3.50.

If you're in Select, you're able to set a seven-day book promotion each 90-day period, reducing your price below $2.99, but still receiving 70%. A .99 book would receive about .70.

If you aren't in Select, that book would earn 35% or about .35. This sounds like a small matter, but thousands of copies of your ebook can sell when you have a .99 promotion with a company like BookBub.

1,000 books sold at .99 with a 35% royalty would earn about $346.

1,000 books sold at .99 with a 70% royalty would earn about $693.

These promotions work with ebooks available on Amazon.com and Amazon.co.uk and are called Kindle Countdown Deals. You can set a single price like .99 or have the promotion to go through several pricing increments. An example of that would be setting the price to drop to .99 then up to $1.99 before returning to full price.

Benefit 2: Price drops to zero.

An author can also reduce her book to zero for five days out of each 90-day enrollment period.

There are those that wonder if this method of promotion is as successful as it once was because devices are filled with previously downloaded, but unread, free books. Readers don't need to spend time deciding whether or not to download a free book.

Benefit 3: Kindle Unlimited (KU) and the Kindle Owners Lending Library (KOLL).

When your book is enrolled in KDP Select, it is automatically in these two programs.

Kindle Unlimited is a paid, subscription service. Someone pays a fee and reads all the books they want. A voracious reader can do well with KU.

An author is paid for each page read out of a fund set for that month. The amount earned per page varies but is usually .40-something per page. If you have 20,000 pages read, you'll earn around $100.

After summer promotions spiked interest, KU provided half of my Amazon income. It's a big carrot on a stick.

KOLL is rarely discussed. This exclusive to Amazon Prime customers' program allows one book borrowed at a time and only one each month. The author is paid per page read as with KU.

If the reader downloaded a book while a book was in either program, the author will be paid for pages read, even if the book is no longer in it.

KDP Select sounds great, right? Keep reading before you decide.

KDP Select's Disadvantages
Disadvantage 1: Exclusivity

You are selling your *ebook* only on Amazon. Remember, this only concerns ebooks. You are not allowed to sell your ebook anywhere else, and you cannot give it away for free anywhere such as on your website or a promotional site. You can post up to 10% of the book, so you can show a sample on your website. You cannot sell your book anywhere else, so you also can't build an audience anywhere else.

By enrolling in Select, you are exclusive to one seller, Amazon. If Amazon finds fault with you or your books and takes down a book or your entire account, you can lose 100% of your income overnight.

While this may seem like a scene from a dystopian fantasy novel, it isn't. This has happened both for people who made an honest mistake in following the rules and for some who Amazon believed had made a mistake, but hadn't. The account is usually, eventually restored.

Disadvantage 2: Genre Matters

Some genres get far more page reads than others. If you're writing in a genre like romance that's littered with voracious readers, you have more opportunities for bigger payouts than someone with a technical manual.

Disadvantage 3: Rules

There are restrictions about when and how you can use the price promotion benefits. The book has to have been in the program for 30 days, the price can't have changed in the previous month or be changed 14 days after, and you can't run one within 14 days of the end of the 90-day period. They say you can run the promotion if you've checked the box to auto-renew, but it wouldn't let me do it once in 2018.

As to the rules as written, there are no exceptions.

Disadvantage 4: Amazon sets all of the rules for selling your books

By being in Select, you give one company authority over your ebooks. If you're in a genre that sells more ebooks than print, you've given up a lot of control.

If you're thinking about trying Select for 90 days, then going wide for a few months before going back into Select, that may not serve you well. Authors who have bounced in and out of Select often say that it's hard to get traction either there or wide. Once you've tested the waters, you may need to stick with one method for a while to see if it's truly working or not.

Growing a career that's wide can take more time, work, and marketing. Those who've done the work often sell a large number of books every month at sellers other than Amazon.

In 2018, I had one series in Select and one that was wide. Starting in 2019, all my books will be wide. As the market changes, I may reconsider.

*If you don't want to be auto-renewed at the end of the 90-day period in KDP Select, go to the KDP site, hover over the three dots by your published book, click on KDP Select Info, and uncheck the box.

Action Step:

- **Decide if you want this book to be in Amazon's KDP Select program.**

FIFTEEN

SHOULD I UPLOAD MY BOOKS MYSELF OR USE AN AGGREGATOR?

In this chapter: The difference between uploading an ebook directly to a vendor or using a third party and the benefits of each.

You may have skipped over one word in the Indie Glossary thinking you'd never need to know it: aggregator. Even if you're considering being exclusive to Amazon, keep reading to know more about aggregators and understand your options.

First, an aggregator is a company you upload your ebook to, which in turn lists it on vendor websites for you and pays you for each sale minus a fee for their efforts.

An author can upload directly to some vendors for maximum income and access, but they can also use an aggregator for other vendors. In a simple process, I upload my book *The Feather Chase* to the aggregator's site and click the places I want *them* to sell this book. I use Draft2Digital for some vendors. Because I use a PC, not a Mac, I can't upload directly to Apple Books, so I need to use an aggregator. I have been going to Barnes & Noble through D2D for a couple of years, but went direct for this book and like their improved process. D2D does give me access to library sales.

Indie authors usually say that everyone's business is different, and you may choose a different way to do something than I would. There are some points that to me have definitive answers.

I'm going to say that you should never use an aggregator to upload to Amazon. Why? There are many reasons.

Direct to Amazon Reason 1:

It's easy to upload it yourself. There's a video of me uploading this book to Amazon (R) to show you how easy it is. If it's simple to upload to, why lose income?

Direct to Amazon Reason 2:

You can directly contact Amazon if you need to have them change a category or make another correction. This is important.

Direct to Amazon Reason 3:

You can advertise with Amazon Marketing. There is a workaround for this, but it's more complicated.

Direct to Amazon Reason 4:

This may be the biggest reason: you can change the price when you want to have a promotion. I can adjust pricing on a book, say *The Chocolate Spy*, setting it to .99 for a few days. The price will change almost immediately. If I use some aggregators, the price will quickly drop. One aggregator in particular, at least at the time this was written, can't do that.

The upside with an aggregator is that it's easy. Upload once. Done. The downsides are that you pay them a percentage for every sale, and the sales stats may not be as good as going direct. All of them allow changes to the book interior file and cover quickly and with no charges, except for IngramSpark. You'll receive a single payment every month instead of payments from each vendor.

These are the major aggregators, those most often discussed among authors I know and on podcasts. There are others and one or more of them may rise to the top this year, so they'll be featured next year.

Note: All of this information is subject to change and it changes often. If something in the pros and cons is important to you, please verify that it hasn't changed before making a choice.

Draft2Digital (D2D)

They take 15% of net royalties (that's the percentage of the total money owed to you for each sale).

Pros:

Excellent customer service with an actual human.

Free ebook formatting tool that creates high-quality books in ebpub and mobi.

Any changes—cover, interior file, prices, description, etc.—can be changed for free and quickly.

You're paid monthly.

Universal Book Links allow you to have one link a reader clicks on that shows all vendors where your ebook is available and it sends them to the correct store for their country. This tool and the formatting tool are free to everyone and you do not have to publish with D2D.

Cons:

None that I can think of other than the fact that you give up some income by using an aggregator.

Smashwords

They were the first aggregator, a pioneer in the self-publishing world.

They take 15% or less of net, estimated at 10% of retail

Pros:

The coupon generator allows you to create a code to give to readers and reviewers for a book that is downloaded from the Smashwords store. The coupon can be for a discount or free and can have an expiration date.

Readers can subscribe to receive author alerts that let them know when a new book releases.

Authors determine the percentage shown as a free sample, but it is up to the vendor to use that percentage.

You can upload a Word file and their "Meatgrinder" tool will format it for you.

Any changes—cover, interior file, prices, description, etc.—can be changed for free and quickly.

Smashwords also has an online store and books bought through that store earn more per copy.

Cons:

Customer service is average.

PublishDrive

In 2018 this company rose to become a favorite among authors. Based in Budapest, PublishDrive sells to a similar list of vendors as Smashwords and D2D, but also works with vendors like China's massive Dangdang.

Takes 10% commission.

In 2018 they introduced an optional subscription model where authors pay a flat fee of $100 each month and receive 100% of the royalties. This would, of course, only benefit an author with high sales volume.

Pros:

Access to Google Play Books.

Can request review copies for marketing from Apple Books, Kobo and Google Play Books.

They offer to help promote your book through their channels if you have a BookBub* Featured Deal. Wow.

They have a program for paid promotion with Google Adwords.

Paid monthly.

Royalties are dependent on the vendor category. It's honestly a bit confusing, but they have a page on their site that shows royalties for each vendor (R).

Cons:

If you use PublishDrive for Amazon know that Amazon will not accept a free book from PublishDrive.

IngramSpark

POD printer IngramSpark is known for their print books and distribution. Some authors choose IngramSpark for their ebooks because it's easy. Upload your print book to them, and they offer you a button to click so they can distribute your ebook. Carefully consider that choice.

Pros:
Initial setup is simple

Cons:
IngramSpark charges the highest percentage of those listed here—25-30%.

The lead time for price changes as of publication is two weeks. The delay for updates makes it impossible to change your price for a promotion for a few days, a common marketing strategy.

They charge a fee for a new interior or cover file.

The company had customer service issues in 2018.

Note: If you read something that mentions Pronoun, they were a short-lived company.

Subscription sites

Many of you will be familiar with Amazon's Kindle Unlimited or the free books that are available if you subscribe to Amazon Prime. There are other companies that charge a subscription fee, and the reader basically checks out books as they would at a library. Authors will be paid based on the number of people who read their books and how much of the book they read.

Scribd is only reached through aggregators including D2D, Smashwords, and PublishDrive.

Playster seems to be best accessed through an aggregator such as D2D or PublishDrive.

24 Symbols can be accessed through aggregators including D2D or PublishDrive.

Kobo Plus, a subscription service only available in Belgium and the Netherlands, can be added by checking a box when setting up a book on Kobo or through aggregators Draft2Digital or StreetLib.

*BookBub (R) is a company that daily sends emails about discounted books, both indie and trad. Authors apply, sometimes multiple times, to be featured. Cost varies by genre and price with free books the least expensive. It can feel like you've won the lottery when you receive an acceptance email. My books always end up number one in their category with a BookBub Featured Deal. There are other companies that offer similar programs, none with the same reach as BookBub, but for a much lower cost.

Action Step:

- **If you've decided to be wide, choose if you will upload directly to a vendor, use an aggregator(s) or both.**

SIXTEEN
HOW DO I TURN A WORD DOC INTO AN EBOOK?

In this chapter: How to create an ebook

Formatting is the process of turning your computer file into a book. When your book is completely edited with the possible exception of a final proofread, you're ready to format your book. You can choose to do this yourself or hire someone to do it.

This chapter is about ebooks, but there's also a chapter about print formatting.

Formatting a book, especially an ebook, is surprisingly simple. A work of fiction is very easy to turn into an ebook. Nonfiction has additional work if there are images, but it's still straightforward. Ebooks can be made in a very basic way with simple chapter headers, or they can be more decorative. In the last couple of years, having decorative elements has become popular.

If you have an illustrated book such as a comic or children's picture book, there are different systems that you'll use, and those specialized steps aren't detailed here.

If you'd prefer, you can hire someone to format your book. It's a good idea to ask other authors for recommendations.

An ebook can be formatted in Word on both free and paid sites. The first three of these common formatting tools are free. Each will create the required table of contents.

Note: Amazon's file type is .mobi. Other sellers use .epub, and you can upload .epub to Amazon.

Ebook Formatting Tool 1:

Draft2Digital's (D2D) free system formats ebooks with decorative elements easily online (no software to download). Books can be downloaded in .epub or .mobi formats. You don't have to sell a book through them to use their formatting tool.

Ebook Formatting Tool 2:

Smashwords uses a conversion tool they call "Meatgrinder" to format the Word doc of a text-only book or a book with "some images." They have a Smashwords Style Guide that gives detailed directions on how to prepare your Word doc for their system. It's specific. The end product may work perfectly, but it won't have decorative flourishes.

Ebook Formatting Tool 3:

Amazon released Kindle Create in 2018. You download the app to your computer, upload the Word file into it, and follow the steps. They have continued to update it, and if you choose to only publish to Amazon, it may be worth trying. In addition to mostly text books, it can also format books with images including comic books.

Ebook Formatting Tool 4:

Vellum is a very popular paid platform. It can only be used with a Mac computer or through a paid site called Mac in Cloud from a PC. You don't have to pay up front; you can format your book to test it out, then pay if you like what you see and want to download it. You can also format your print book with them. I used Vellum for the first time with this book and liked the fact that it made ebook and print at the same time.

Ebook Formatting Tool 5: You can choose to use a template for your print book formatting from Book Design Templates, and it will also format your ebook (see the Print chapter).

To see how your ebook will look, you can check it out with two free apps: Kindle Previewer (R) for .mobi files and Adobe Digital Editions (R) for .epub files. Once both apps are your computer, you can click on the file, and the correct app will open.

Tip: You may need to know about a Word function called Styles. If the chapters or another element aren't showing up correctly when you use one of the formatting tools, you can easily go back to Word and add Styles, which are pre-made formatting instructions that the formatting tool should read. I'd never paid attention to this feature until I began formatting my ebooks in Word. Chapter titles can be standardized by simply highlighting a title's text and clicking on

"Heading 1" from the boxes at the top of the screen. Do that with each of the chapter titles, and they'll all read correctly to the formatting tool. Don't assume you need to do this because you may not. If you do need it, Google how to use Styles in your version of Word.

Action steps:

- **Choose a book formatting method or hire an interior formatter.**
- **Check the formatted book in Kindle Previewer and/or Adobe Digital Editions.**

Now that you have a formatted book, or someone is formatting it for you, we'll talk about the things you'll need to know to upload your book for sale. It's straightforward if you take it a step at a time. We'll do this in the order Amazon's KDP site does

SEVENTEEN
HOW DO I WRITE THE WORDS ON THE BACK COVER AND THE ONLINE SALES COPY?

In this chapter: Create words that can help sell your book online and on a book

The words describing your book at Amazon and elsewhere, and often also the words on the back of your print book, are one of your most important marketing tools for a book. An online shopper usually sees the cover, clicks to the book's page to read the sales copy, and makes the decision to buy or not. (They may continue to the "Look inside" or open the physical book, so the book itself has to hold up to scrutiny too.)

This small piece of text goes by many names including:

Back Cover Copy (BCC)

Book Blurb

Book Description

Book Sales Copy

Book Page Copy

Even though it's not always on a physical book,

"back cover copy" is used by many, so I'll use that and sales copy interchangeably.

BCC can convince a potential reader that out of the many books they have to choose from, *yours* is the one to buy.

So, we know these words are important. You shouldn't write this late one night because your book cover designer says he needs it by morning.

Looking at successful books is helpful with many of the steps in the self-publishing process. When it comes to back cover copy, you can study trad books, but keep in mind that tradition often rules when they're writing it. Indies are sometimes faster than trad to adapt and learn new techniques.

When I wrote my first back cover copy, I copied trad. A couple of years later, I discovered a completely new way to write back cover copy. Successful indie authors realize that they're selling a product. That makes back cover copy more involved than a mere summary.

It's advertising sales copy.

Just like an ad for bacon or aspirin, your back cover copy exists to sell something: your book.

Unless you have an established following with a substantial mailing list, this is one of your top ways to find potential readers.

When you search for examples to study, look for high-ranking self-published authors.

Don't forget that this sales copy is one of the

important steps between "Do I care?" and "I'm buying this book."

Set aside a day to write the back cover copy. You're busy, you say. You're on the home stretch. You're almost ready to hit publish on your book. Take the time.

Write this. Make it better. Make it better still.

I'm continually improving BCC, making it the best it can be. The Resources page (R) has links to examples of good BCC.

The most important point is that this should *never be a summary*. First, that can be boring. Second, you want to entice the reader but not give away too much. This is especially important with fiction.

In nonfiction, what problem, known as a "pain point," will you resolve by the end of the book? What will the reader know that they didn't know before? How to build a deck? How to stay calm while writing advertising copy?

You want to build excitement for your book. You're going to use different writing skills for marketing than you do for writing a book.

If you think of this as fun, maybe even a fun challenge, you'll enjoy this more. Going into this—or any project—believing it will be scary, overwhelming, and impossible won't give the best results. Take a deep breath, say "I can do this," and put on your advertising hat.

There are some "rules" to help you. Rules are in quotation marks because experts sometimes break the rules. Follow the rules until you're an expert.

Begin with a headline. Don't begin with a long block of text. Hold the reader's hand and pull them step-by-step through the copy from beginning to end.

Don't state the obvious. "In this romance . . ."

Don't say your book is the best thing ever. Near the end, give examples of books similar to yours. If they like _____, then they'll love _____ (your book.)

At the end, always have a call to action—ask them to buy the book.

"Fall in love with Jemma and Nathaniel. Begin reading *Falling for Alaska* today."

"Ready to get your book published? Click to start *Self-Publishing Secrets* now!"

You don't want to give away the point of the book or the plot in the BCC. You want to intrigue the reader, make them want to read more. Remember—I can't tell you this too many times—you're promoting your book.

Rewrite your back cover copy until it sparkles. I find it's best to let it sit a day or two and come back to it. Sometimes I like what I've written. Sometimes it's trash, and I need to start over.

Your print book cover won't need a call to action. It will be slightly different. If you're doing print now, make a few changes to your online version so that it can work for both, or use two slightly different versions.

One of the best things about this process is that your book description isn't written in stone. Online, this can be changed any time you want. You can test one version, see if it helps the book sell, then change it up if needed, and try another version. You're the boss.

It's harder to change what's on the back of a print book because your cover designer is involved, so I try to write something for the print version that's clear and stick with it.

Action Steps:

- **Review competitor's online sales copy.**
- **Write a draft version of your sales copy.**
- **Revise it for your print book if you're doing print now.**
- **Refine both.**

EIGHTEEN
WHAT ARE KEYWORDS?

In this chapter: What goes in vendor's keywords and categories sections

One of the new things you'll need to learn is how to use keywords. What are they? Keywords are words or phrases that searchers use to find something online. Whatever you enter into Google or Pinterest for a search is a keyword.

Keywords are important in publishing because they guide readers to your book. When you upload your book to Amazon's KDP for ebooks, you'll fill in seven blanks with carefully chosen keyword phrases.

If you're like me in the beginning, you'll fill in the blanks with the most obvious things that come to mind.

Keywords done right can drive sales. Done poorly, they're words in blanks that not only don't help you but can cause your book to be in the wrong category.

The most important thing to know about these keywords is that Amazon is a search engine, just as

Google is a search engine. People go to Amazon and type what they're looking for in the blank. Type anything slowly in the Amazon search bar and you'll see it autofill, probably with a list of options. Those options are all keywords.

To find your keywords, go to Amazon and type in what you think would bring up books like yours. I just typed in "sweet romance in Alaska" and much to my surprise, my Christmas novella was the third book down. Yay!

Finding keywords isn't something you spend ten minutes on as you're uploading your book to Amazon and arrive at that place on the page. You're going to spend some time on this, probably an hour or two. Yes, keywords are that important, but before you hyperventilate because it's one more thing you have to do, know that you can change them at any time, and changes in Amazon happen quickly. Do your best now, but if you mess it up, it's fixable.

You'll need to use an incognito window on your computer, so Amazon isn't simply filling in the blanks on what they know you like. I use the Chrome browser and find the incognito window by clicking on the three dots in the upper right corner.

You can dig much more deeply into keywords once your book is published and you have extra time. You'll get solid keywords though by just searching on Amazon.

Don't choose a word or two alone. It's better to use what's known as a long tail keyword. These are keywords with multiple words, so I wouldn't use "romance" or even "sweet romance" as keywords. "Small town sweet romance" should be better, but as I was typing it, that didn't autofill. Remember to type slowly so you give autofill time to populate. You want search terms that autofill because those are what people are using to search. "Small town romance" does autofill.

Click on the search term, and when the window opens, see how many results it shows. It has a decent sized-audience of 30,000, so it's a keeper. Alaska romance has 1,000. That makes it a smaller category and easier to rise to the first page in it, but there aren't as many people searching for it.

To make my keyword into an even longer long-tail keyword, I can add "neighbor" because they're neighbors and some people enjoy books like that. This doesn't mean the shorter keyword won't sell books, but a longer keyword can potentially reach more readers.

Beware that you can't use any words that are part of your title, subtitle or series name. I shouldn't use Alaska as a keyword because Amazon already has that since it's in the series name. You also can't use another author's name or book title. And you *want* to include certain keywords to be in certain categories. Amazon has a list of those (R).

There is a tool for this and other similar things, the app KDP Rocket (R), if you want to splurge.

Once you have your Amazon keywords, use them on the other vendor and/or aggregator sites too. Keywords will be important if you decide to advertise with Amazon Ads. That list of keywords can begin with these, but it will be larger.

Categories is the next thing you'll enter on Amazon. Choose the categories that books like yours are in, but know that some categories aren't available here. My romances are in the Clean & Wholesome category, but that isn't a choice at set-up. When your book is live (published), you can contact Amazon and ask them to put your book in those categories. Get as close as you can.

Action Steps:

- **Research keywords.**
- **Create a list of keywords that might suit your book.**
- **Refine the list to seven keywords, making sure they're long-tail keywords.**
- **Choose your book's categories.**

NINETEEN

SHOULD I SET UP A PRE-ORDER FOR MY EBOOK?

In this chapter: Whether or not you want to sell your ebook before the release date

As you upload your book to ebook sellers, you may notice an option to have it go live immediately or as quickly as they process a new book or pre-order. This discussion is *only* about ebooks.

A pre-order is exactly as it sounds. A book is shown on a vendor's site, say Amazon, and it has a future publication date. The author sets the date in advance, knowing when his or her book will be ready to be uploaded.

Your book can be sold before the actual release date.

Sounds easy, right? Like a great idea. Why wouldn't you want to do that?

Well, there are authors on both sides of this option.

If you finish your books well in advance, are certain they will be edited, proofread, and formatted long before the date, you may be interested in pre-orders.

On the other hand, if this is your first self-published book, everything's feeling a bit overwhelming, and you don't know an exact date for the completion of all those tasks, please don't select pre-order. Stress, sometimes a lot of stress, lies on the road ahead if you do.

You may wonder how you upload a not-quite-ready book for pre-order? Some vendors allow assetless pre-orders, meaning that the asset, the book, doesn't have to be uploaded.

There is a deadline for submission with each vendor, the number of days before release that you're required to meet, and there are sometimes stiff penalties for missing it.

Some people believe pre-orders are great for building buzz about your book. You'll have to decide what works best for you.

To set up a pre-order, you will need the basics about your book including the book description. A temporary book cover can be used for most if not all of these vendors, but do you want a less-than-amazing book cover out there?

Some people use a "dummy" file, one that isn't for the book you're listing. That can work with some vendors and not for others. Be careful with this.

All of this information is subject to change. Double-check the details before setting up your pre-order.

Amazon

Pre-orders up 90 days before release.

Amazon requires the book's text file and cover when listing. Many upload a not-ready interior file because an updated file can be uploaded later. A temporary cover can be uploaded and changed later. There's no "Look inside" feature before publication date.

You must upload the final file more than three days before release.

Customers pay the price when they ordered even if you raise the price before release. If you drop the price, they pay the lower price.

The company bans you from pre-orders for a year if you miss your release date or postpone your release the allowed 30 days or less, or cancel the pre-order. That's actually fair because Amazon offered a product to customers, they bought it and expected to receive it on that date. The customer believes Amazon failed them; most don't know about the behind-the-scenes author goof-up.

Apple Books

Pre-orders up to one year before release.

Asset-less pre-orders with no interior or cover file required, but a book without a cover probably won't generate interest unless you're a superstar.

Allows a partial book with chapters or an excerpt that the reader will see. This is a great promo opportunity.

Files need to be uploaded at least 10 days prior to release.

Apple Books warns that you may not be able to do asset-less pre-orders in the future if you miss the date.

Barnes & Noble Press

Pre-orders up to 12 months before release.

Customers are charged the price on the day they ordered the book, it won't go up or down if you change the price.

Asset-less allowed. If you choose to upload the beginning of the book, instead of the full manuscript, it will be visible, not hidden until release.

A temporary book cover can be used.

Upload the final cover and interior file before 72 hours of publication.

Kobo

Pre-orders set as early as you choose.

The online platform doesn't track pre-order sales, but you can email them and ask for the numbers.

Upload the first three chapters of the book because they will show in a preview.

The customer is charged the lowest price if you raise or drop the price before release.

GooglePlay

Their rules differ by country so you'll need to check.

Pre-orders up to a year before release.

They require a cover and at least four pages of the manuscript. If you upload the complete file, you can allow previews before release. Sample pages can be blocked from preview by the checking the "No Preview Before On Sale Date" box.

The customer will be charged the lower price if you drop the price after ordering.

Pre-Orders through aggregators

Draft2Digital, Smashwords, and PublishDrive all offer pre-orders. (D2D doesn't offer Amazon pre-orders.) The rules through an aggregator should be similar to if not exactly the same as the rules when going direct.

Action Step:

- **Decide if your book should be for sale on pre-order or wait until release date.**

TWENTY
DO I WANT DRM?

In this chapter: Whether or not to choose DRM for your ebooks

DRM stands for Digital Rights Management. It is supposed to protect the book against being copied and against piracy. The reality is that DRM can be stripped from a book fairly easily. Google "remove DRM" for examples.

DRM is optional at Amazon, Apple Books, Kobo, Google Play, and Barnes & Noble Press. Major aggregators vary: Draft2Digital has a checkbox you can use to apply DRM to your entire catalog of books, Smashwords and PublishDrive don't use DRM.

This is a bigger decision than you may think because once a book is published, you can change almost anything except DRM. If you change your mind, the one solution seems to be to unpublish your book and republish it with a different title, not choosing DRM that time.

Some sites such as Amazon offer the author the choice of having DRM on their book or not. Amazon books with DRM can only be read on a Kindle app, and that may frustrate some of your readers.

This is one of those things that *sounds* like a good idea. The actual story is that book pirates know how to strip DRM from your book. You may also be upsetting some readers and potential readers because it limits sharing of the book.

As usual, it is your choice, but go into it without the fear of piracy, and see it from a reader's perspective. I started out using DRM, then learned more about it and didn't use it with later books. But your experience and decisions may be different.

Action Step:

- **Decide if you want DRM for this book.**

TWENTY-ONE
DO I NEED A PUBLISHING HOUSE NAME?

In this chapter: Whether or not you want a publisher name

You do not need to have a publishing house name. It completely depends on your publishing goals and your vision for your business.

When you upload to Amazon's KDP, there's an optional blank for "Publisher." An author can use her own name as the publisher, choose a publishing house name, or simply leave it blank. On some sites such as Draft2Digital, they will automatically use your author name if you leave it blank.

Some successful authors do have a publishing company name; others do not.

I wanted my books to look like traditionally published books, so I chose to have a publishing company name. If someone asks who publishes my books, I can answer either that I self-published or give that name.

If you choose a name, search on Google to make

sure it isn't already being used. In the US, you can also search the trademark database.

Check with your state or other governing body or a lawyer to see how and if you should register this as a DBA (Doing Business As) name.

Action Step:

- **Decide if you will use your name, create a publishing company name, or leave the blank empty.**

TWENTY-TWO
HOW DO I CHOOSE MY BOOK'S PRICE?

In this chapter: Steps to price your book

When it's time to set a price for your book, first check out your competition.

For ebooks, price them in line with other indie authors. Some trad publishers set ebook prices high, sometimes close to the price of a print book.

You may not sell as many ebooks at a higher price, but you can certainly test it. You're looking for the best income from book sales. That sounds obvious, but it's mentioned so you don't get caught up in setting the highest possible price. A higher volume can make up for a lower price, but some authors are doing well recently with somewhat higher prices.

What is the range of prices that books such as your sell for? Click on some of the lowest priced books to see if they're doing a temporary promotion. You need the regular price.

If you're a new author, it may be a good idea to not

start with the highest price. Also, Amazon has a tool that you can use as you set up a book where they recommend a price for similar books. Consider that.

When you've chosen a price and set it, watch to see what happens.

For print, follow the same process, but keep in mind the upfront costs for printing and the discount to stores. Always give yourself a profit. If you're doing print and using IngramSpark (*much* more on this later), be cautious about putting a price in your barcode because changing the price later will mean you need to upload a new version of the cover.

Action Steps:

- **Check similar books to see prices.**
- **Choose your book's price.**

TWENTY-THREE

SHOULD MY BOOK BE IN PRINT?

In this chapter: Whether or not you need print and how to have it printed if you do

When an author says "print," they usually mean a paperback book. A small percentage start out with hardcover, so this isn't a hard and fast rule, but paperback is typical.

Your book is most likely in Word. Turning that Word doc into a print book takes more steps than an ebook. I've formatted all of my books, but it has a learning curve.

With that in mind, let's first look at whether or not you even *need* a print book in the beginning. And print isn't instead of ebooks; it's in addition to them.

As with other parts of the process, print book sales depend in part on the genre.

Nonfiction tends to sell well in print.

Children's books sell well in print. I outsell print to

ebook for my kids' mysteries and believe it's because parents and grandparents prefer print.

Popular fiction genres such as romance, mysteries, and sci fi don't generally sell as well in print. You'll often sell thousands of ebooks to a handful of print.

There are exceptions, but consider the above a starting point. Audiobook sales are rising, so you may want to consider them as your next step instead of print if you're in one of those fiction genres. But if you're a lover of paper books like me, you'll probably have print go live about the same time as the ebook.

Some say in a commanding voice that you should have your book in all formats from day one. Good idea. But maybe too much to take on with a first book. Do what makes sense for you.

If you've decided you need print, then keep reading. If not, save this chapter and the next two for later and move on.

POD or Offset?

Your next decision about print books is how they'll be printed. If the majority of your books will be sold by someone other than you either online or at a store, you'll want to use Print-On-Demand (POD).

With this business model, the author uploads a book interior file and cover to the printer's website. Then when an order is placed on Amazon or elsewhere, the book is printed, they ship it and pay you. POD printers can print one book at a time or hundreds. The cost per book will be slightly higher for this service, but there is no charge to have the books listed for sale on Amazon and other booksellers.

Offset printers can print hundreds or thousands of copies of a book for less money per copy, but you have to store them *and* get them to the seller. About thirty average-sized books fit in a box, so picture the number of boxes you'd have for only 500 books—more than sixteen. *If* you plan to sell hundreds of books a year at events or from the back of the room after speaking, this could be a viable option for you. Oh, and if you have the storage space or are willing to rent a climate-controlled storage area.

There will be many printers to choose from if you're going with offset. Get samples from each to make sure you like their work.

Amazon currently has two programs for selling the books you've had printed, both with fees.

If you'll be hand-selling hundreds of books and selling online, then the good news is that you could have your books printed POD *and* offset, getting the best of both. Print as many books as you'll hand-sell and upload your book to a POD printer for online and store sales. But you'll still have a guest room filled with books. That's okay. Grandma can squeeze around them when she comes to visit.

When it comes to POD, there are two main choices: Amazon's KDP and IngramSpark.

KDP

Note: You may read in books or online about using Amazon's CreateSpace for print books. In 2018, books in CreateSpace migrated to KDP, the former ebook-only arm of Amazon. One page now shows sales of both KDP ebooks and print, and that's good news. There are subtle differences between the old and new companies and some growing pains which will hopefully be ironed out during 2019. KDP is your only choice with an Amazon-owned company, but not your only choice.

Pros:

Your new book with no proven track record can show as In Stock on Amazon.

They can print color, but it's expensive. A 6" x 9" 200-page book on 60lb paper would cost $14.85 to print with Amazon (R). The same book at IngramSpark (R) would cost $5.94 on 50lb paper or $7.44 on 70lb paper.

Cons:

The discount rate, the percentage off sales price which impacts the money earned, is set by Amazon. The authors sets the price, it's the amount deducted from that price they don't choose.

Print quality, especially the book cover's colors, can be inconsistent. A print proof (the author's sample of the book) can be perfect, but a box of books may not have the correct colors, or vice versa. While I've heard authors talk about this, I've never had a reader mention a problem.

Amazon offers Expanded Distribution to reach booksellers outside Amazon. Many find they receive a small royalty from books sold in that program, and it's thought that bookstores don't want to buy from any platform tied to their biggest competitor, Amazon.

IngramSpark
Pros:

Print quality is excellent.

Many, many trim sizes (the finished size of the book) are available.

Color and hardcover are options.

IngramSpark is part of the massive Ingram distribution company, so your book can be sold in many places in the world.

The author sets the discount rate (the percentage off for sellers vs. the percentage you keep).

Cons:

Some updates such as price changes are only made monthly. If you want to change the price on March 1, it won't go into effect until near the end of the month.

In 2018, IngramSpark's success overwhelmed their customer service. Ingram is working to improve it, so 2019 may be better. Tip: According to customer service reps I spoke with while at Ingram, the best ways to contact them are to phone near the time they open in the morning or use chat if you don't get through on the phone.

There are occasional print errors because of their high volume. When that's happened, and it's been rare, they've replaced the books. I've never had a reader complain, so it's infrequent. Ingram offered a tip when I was there: Choose 6" x 9" or 5.5" x 8.5" as your trim size because they print that size most often; their machines don't have to switch to a less common size, so there's less potential for error. Don't worry if you're in love with another size though.

Can't decide? Good news! You can choose one of these companies or use both to maximize the benefits.

IngramSpark reaches markets around the globe and for a fairly consistent royalty per sale. When you also add Amazon, you keep Ingram's distribution, and your book almost always shows as In Stock on Amazon. Amazon prints the books ordered on their site. Ingram prints the others. Ingram may also print the Amazon books because Amazon outsources printing and Ingram is one of the printers they use.

Other POD printers

There are other POD printers, but at this time, they don't offer the same terms. Barnes & Noble Press now prints paperbacks and hardcover, both in black and white and color. The books can be sold through Barnes & Noble online, but not elsewhere. And like Amazon, they set the discount rate, choosing the usual bookstore rate of 55%, which can cut into an author's profits.

These are the main choices, but if you're someone who's heard about Lulu or Blurb and want to know more, keep reading. Lulu can print and distribute your book, but sales through Amazon and other major sellers bring a small profit per book. You can link to Lulu with Shopify and sell books directly from your website with a decent return on each book, if that's something you'd like to explore. Blurb is another option, but the cost per book is higher and using their business model means you have additional fees when selling on Amazon.

Action Steps:

- Decide if you want print now, later, or never.
- If you do want print, choose to start with POD or offset.
- If you choose POD, which company will you use?

TWENTY-FOUR
FORMATTING A PRINT BOOK

In this chapter: How to turn a Word document into a print book

There are additional steps to take if you want a professional-quality print book. Remember, that's what aiming for here, quality—not the "self-published" book some expect to see.

You'll need to format your book again in a different way than with an ebook. Then you'll need to upload it to the company that will print it and order a proof (sample) copy to approve. This isn't hard to do; it just has more steps than an ebook.

I prefer to format my print book first, then, when it's as perfect as I can make it, I format my ebook. That's backward from what many do so in this book I went with the most common method and had you do ebooks first. Go with what works for you.

With your ebook, you stripped out any formatting.

Reading an ebook is all about the reader's choices—the font, size of text, spacing between lines, justified right (text lining up on the right side as it does on the left)—these are all things the reader can choose to change on their device.

A print book is exactly as *you* want it to be every time. The choice of book size, font, spacing, and justification all matter. Each of the choices is about making the book attractive and/or more readable. Readability is important. If you hire someone to format your book—a professional, experienced someone—then they already know this.

I formatted my first book in Adobe InDesign, the next six in Word, and this one in Vellum. I created the journal in the free Canva app.

You *can* format your own books. There are quite a few options for doing this, or you can pay someone to do it for you.

InDesign

InDesign (R) creates a high-quality book. It's also professional-level software and at the time of this writing $20.99 per month. If you're a student or teacher, they have special first-year pricing. I've used computers for many years, so I'm okay with technology. Even so, I had to watch a video series that took me through the process. If tech stresses you out, keep reading because there are easier options.

I didn't want to keep paying for InDesign, so I started formatting my books in Word which creates a book that's about 98% as awesome as InDesign. The differences would only, maybe, be noticed by a professional graphic designer.

Templates

Templates can be a good option. I bought a template to use for my second book, the first I made in Word, to simplify the process. You can find templates free and for purchase online, including from Amazon. I used one from The Book Designer (R), tweaked what I wanted, and liked the results, so I used it for the whole series. I didn't use a template for books two and three of my other series because I knew how to format in Word by then.

A template sets the margins around the sides of the page, has correct gutter spacing—that's the inside of the page, the side that's glued to the spine. You want the book to be easily read and not have text tucked too far into the glued area. Don't you hate when you have to bend a book so you can read it?

A template will have page numbers, running heads —the book title, etc. at the top of each page—all set up for you. A quality one will also have the copyright page set up for you, so you just change it to your IBSN, etc.

Vellum

Vellum is a paid app that is becoming more and more popular. This app is also mentioned in the ebook formatting chapter because it can do both ebook and print. It's Mac-only and I use a PC, so I have to access it through a site called MacinCloud. There is a one-time fee for using Vellum, either ebook alone or ebook and print. One thing I love about Vellum is that it automatically fixes widows and orphans (defined below). It also adds chapter page numbers to a table of contents—a plus for nonfiction authors.

Hire an expert

You can hire someone to do this for you. The cost to format a text-only book shouldn't be too high. When many images, footnotes, or other special touches, the time it takes the formatter goes up and so will the cost.

What goes where?

I mentioned the copyright page earlier. It's important to also mention that a print book's format has been set for a very long time. Pick up a few books and flip through the first pages, what's known as the "front matter."

There are some options for the first pages of the book. A book can begin with reviews, an excerpt from the book, or a "half title" page—that's a page with the title and sometimes the subtitle and/or series name.

If there are other books in a series, that list will go on the back of the half title page or excerpt, or the last page of the reviews.

The title always goes on a right-hand page. It will have not only the title, subtitle and/or series name but also the author's name along with the publisher's name and logo.

The copyright page is the reverse side of the title page (known as "verso"), so on a left page. This page will have the copyright notice, ISBN, and other information you may choose to put there such as your cover designer's name.

The dedication, if you want to use one, is on the page to the right of the copyright page. Otherwise, there will be a blank page there.

The actual first page of the book and the page numbering can begin on the next *right* page.

Correct formatting

Correctly formatting a book also includes taking care of widows and orphans. In book formatting, these are parts of sentences. If you flip through a traditionally published book, you'll see that there isn't a half sentence at the top of a page. It breaks the reader's concentration when he gets to the end of a paragraph and has to look to the top of the next page or flip the page to finish it. Major publishers fix that when they format, and you will too.

Publishers also fix sentences that wrap to the next line and have only one word on that line. This is done either manually by adjusting the space between letters, rewriting it a bit (I find some of my best improvements are made as I format), or with a system such as Vellum that takes care of widows and orphans.

Check to make sure all pages have the same number of lines on them. Occasionally, this will be something you need to correct.

If you pay a professional formatter to do your book, the formatter should do it to these specs even without your mentioning it. If you format it yourself or use someone new to book publishing, you'll need to pay attention to the set formula. It's pretty basic, but getting it wrong makes a book scream self-published.

Font

Fonts are serif or sans serif. The serif is the small foot that sticks off the ends of the letters in some fonts. Times New Roman is a well-known example. Sans means without in French, so a sans serif font doesn't have those extra bits on letters and is considered to have a more modern look. Arial is a common sans serif font.

Print books are usually made with serif fonts, partly because they're believed to be easier to read and partly because it's tradition. Unless you have a unique project, choose a serif font for the main text of your book.

If you're using a formatting app such as Vellum, you will have their choice of fonts and that's fine. I had unlimited font choices with the methods I used with my books. I've often used the free font Gandhi Serif for my print book interiors and its related font Gandhi Sans for other details in those books.

Fonts aren't randomly chosen; they're chosen for a reason. Gandhi is a very readable font, and it is more condensed than many other fonts. More words fit on the printed page, but it doesn't feel cramped, so that saves me pages in the print book and money since I'm charged per page for POD printing.

Only use fonts for which you have the commercial rights. Fonts can be free or cost money. I check free sites first and always read the rights before choosing a font.

Your Photo

You may be wondering if you should have a photo on the back cover. Many books are sold online now, not chosen by a person standing in a store and flipping a book to the back to see who wrote it. A photo on the back of the book probably isn't necessary for that reason. If you know you'll be hand-selling books at events or bookstores, this may be a good addition.

Uploading

Getting your book on Amazon or IngramSpark is a matter of following the steps. It's free to publish with Amazon. IngramSpark charges a fee, but there's often a coupon. Before uploading, check the file specifications and save the book's file in the specified way. Always follow the specifications *exactly*.

You've already chosen your trim size. When you're uploading your book, you'll make some other choices, most of them similar to what you did for your ebook. Print options include:

Paper color:

Cream is for fiction. Nonfiction is often on white. Stick with the custom when you're new.

Binding Type:

Choose Perfect Bound for a regular paperback book.

BISAC Code:

This stands for Book Industry Standards and Communications, but no one will know it beyond BISAC. Your choice will tell everyone selling your book what categories it belongs in so choose wisely.

Contributors:

You alone are the contributor unless this is an anthology or something like that. Your paid editor is not a contributor. I occasionally see that mistake on an

Amazon listing. Mention them on your copyright page or in Acknowledgments if you feel the need.

Keywords:

See Keyword chapter.

After uploading

Amazon and IngramSpark will email when the eproof is ready. This is a PDF that looks like your printed book. Please preview that PDF and go through it from the front cover to the back, flipping every page to make sure it looks right. DO NOT approve the eproof for publication. This is your first check.

Order a print proof of the book. Why, you ask? You checked it, and it looked good. One important reason is that you want to make sure the cover prints properly, that the colors are correct. I had a book cover with the colors off, so my designer had to tweak it.

Did the interior print well and is the gutter, the space toward the spine, working well for reading?

When you've received the print proof, you'll want to read the entire book from beginning to end. Whoa. Read it again? Yes. This is the final check to make sure nothing was missed. It's great that you had editors and beta readers, but this is your final quality check. I've caught a few mistakes at this point, and it surprises me every time, but I'm grateful for the chance to fix before them before it's live.

Once you've gone through these steps, either approve the book for future or present publication or upload a new file. When I've uploaded a new file, but had only minor changes to the text such as fixing a typo, I won't order a new proof. If the errors are on the cover or the formatting, I will order a new one before approving. It's another step, but you're in business and this is your product. You want your book to be the best it can be. Go through the steps and know that you've done your best.

Action Steps:

- **Choose how you will format your book.**
- **If you're formatting it yourself, choose the method. If you've hired someone, skip the next two steps.**
- **Choose your font(s).**
- **Format your book.**
- **Upload your book.**
- **Review the eproof.**
- **Order a print proof and review it.**
- **Publish.**

TWENTY-FIVE
DO I NEED AN LCCN?

In this chapter: What an LCCN is and whether or not you want one

An LCCN (R) is the Library of Congress Control Number, and like the ISBN, it goes on your copyright page. This is only for *print* books in the US. Many but not all books from major publishers have one.

From the Library of Congress website:

"The publisher prints the control number in the book and thereby facilitates cataloging and other book processing activities. The PCN links the book to any record which the Library of Congress, other libraries, bibliographic utilities, or book vendors may create."

This is an identification number that the Library of Congress assigns to each book it has cataloged. You apply for a Preassigned Control Number (PCN) and are sent an LCCN. It has nothing to do with copyright.

You go to the website, enter your information, and

receive an email with your number. My last one arrived the same business day.

The LCCN for Falling for Alaska is shown on the copyright page as LCCN: 2015918278.

The LCCN in a traditionally published book will usually have additional information along with the number. That CIP (Cataloging in Publication) data is basically what you would have found on a card in an old-fashioned card catalog, for those who still remember them. The bibliographic data is supplied by the Library of Congress—for publishers who've published books by at least three authors which "were widely acquired by libraries."

That leaves you out. But there are companies you can pay to create the information for you. Search for "CIP data self-publishing" to find options if you want to add that extra section of information.

Note: A planned change to this system will take place sometime in 2019. Please check their site for updates.

You are required to mail a copy of the book immediately upon publication.

I have applied for and used an LCCN with my books from the beginning. I've never had anyone who bought a book mention the number.

Will this help sales? Maybe, but maybe not. Your book will look correct to a library, but they will see that *after* purchasing it. If you had fit the regular category for applying and the Library of Congress created the data block for you, that would be sent to libraries and might generate sales. This falls into the category of maybe and why not?, so I use LCCNs and will probably continue to use them.

Action Steps:

- **Decide if you do or do not want an LCCN.**
- **Order an LCCN if you want one.**

TWENTY-SIX
DO I HAVE TO BUY A BARCODE?

In this chapter: Why you probably don't need to buy a barcode

A barcode is the series of lines with numbers in a box on the back of a print book. This is *only* for print books.

The usual question is, "Where should I buy a barcode?" There are places online that will sell you a barcode and places where you can make one for free. But you probably don't need to do either.

If you use one of the two major POD printers, Amazon's KDP or IngramSpark, they will provide a free barcode. The two companies have different systems for getting your free barcode.

Amazon

They put a barcode in a 2" by 1.2" white box in the lower right-hand corner of the back cover .25 from the spine and trimmed edge of the book. Their barcode will cover any decorative element that's already there. Yes, you can use your own barcode, but it has to meet the same specs, or they'll redo it. Amazon's barcode is placed by them after your cover is made and submitted to them.

IngramSpark

They'll provide a free barcode when the cover is uploaded to their free template. You'll go online (R), enter your ISBN number, the exact page count, paper type, black & white or color, and more. Then they'll create the template and email it as a PDF or InDesign file to you or your designer. IngramSpark is more flexible for the placement; the barcode box can be moved as long as it stays on the back cover and the size doesn't change.

With either company, you can choose to put the retail price into the barcode, but it's always a five-digit code; there would always be another digit at the front. $19.95 would be 51995. For those expecting to sell their book in retail stores, this still could be helpful.

So, who does need to buy a barcode?

You can provide your own barcode for an Amazon book or for IngramSpark.

If you're going to use a traditional offset printer for boxes of books to be sold at events or back of the room, you will need to have a cover with a barcode. If the printed book will *never* be sold by anyone but you, you may not need one, but your book also won't look like a traditionally published book.

If you want an actual price and prefer to have it look like a price—ex. in USD $19.95 instead of 51995—buy a barcode. I've always been content with the free barcode.

Action Steps:

- **Decide whether or not the free barcode will work for you.**
- **Buy a barcode if that's your choice.**

TWENTY-SEVEN

HOW DO I GET MY BOOK INTO LIBRARIES AND BOOKSTORES?

In this chapter: Find out if and how you can reach libraries and bookstores

Almost all authors dream of having their book on bookstore and library shelves. We love books after all, so our books should be where people find them. If you're one of those authors (I was), read on.

Quality with some self-published books, or the lack thereof, is part of the problem with libraries and bookstores. *Self-Publishing Secrets* is showing you how to publish a *quality* book. That's the theme here. I know that's been mentioned several times already, but many, many indie books are poorly written, edited, formatted and/or have homemade-looking covers. That is the expectation when you say "self-published" to whoever buys books at a library or bookstore. You're going to have to make the case that your books are high quality.

If you've chosen to print books only through Amazon, it's also possible that some libraries and bookstores won't order your book. I've heard stories saying both yes and no on this.

Libraries

Libraries are often bound up in tradition when it comes to buying books. There's a system in place. The acquiring librarians read advance reviews in publications like *Publishers Weekly*, *Kirkus,* and *Library Journal*. They also track books winning major awards and on best seller lists. Book orders are often based on these things.

You can now submit your indie book to *Publishers Weekly* through their Booklife site (R). They have a six–twelve week lead time—if they choose your book for review.

Kirkus, with a seven–nine week lead time, allows you to pay (quite a lot) for a review, but paid reviews may or may not help you. A paid review colors the impression it gives through the assumption that it's favorable because you gave them money. But a positive review isn't guaranteed.

Library Journal (R) requires that they receive the book at least three months before publication. Few indie authors hold an unpublished, finished book that long.

If your book fits the reviewer's needs, submit it. It can be a very good thing if it's chosen. Just know that a positive review isn't guaranteed with any of them.

Standard advice about libraries is to donate a book to your local library. Before you do that, contact them to see what will happen with that book. At my library, donated books go into a book sale, not on the shelf.

So, this isn't positive and I know that. You *can* amp up the likelihood that your book will be purchased by libraries.

Reaching libraries idea 1:

Get into a juried event. There's a major book event in my city, the Southern Festival of Books, that's juried, meaning a submitted book is reviewed before the author is invited to participate. Being able to say I participated in that event helped break down some barriers. Someone in authority said I had a quality book and that made it worth buying. This is not the same as an event where you buy a table so you can sit and sell books.

Reaching libraries idea 2:

A book with local or regional interest might be accepted if you talk to someone at the library. It could be worth your time to make phone calls to librarians in that area. Your library may order your book because you're a local author. Mine wouldn't until I was in the juried event.

Reaching libraries idea 3:

I have spent days on the phone cold calling libraries, and I've sold some books. It's a time-consuming process, but if you love libraries like I love libraries, it's something to consider. For every library, you have to go their website to see if they have a stated process for authors to submit purchase requests. You also need to see if they have the acquisitions librarian listed with contact information. If not, see if there's someone listed who is in charge of the section of the library where your book would fit—adult, children's, etc. If still not, call their main number and tell them that you're an author with a _____ (nonfiction about X, romance novel, children's mystery, etc.) book and would like to speak with whomever purchases those books for the library.

Ebooks

Your fantasy about books on library shelves is probably about paperbacks or hardcover, but recently library ebook doors have opened and authors who aren't exclusive to Amazon can sell ebooks to them with Overdrive, Bibliotheca, and Baker & Taylor.

If you've checked out an ebook through a library, you may be familiar with Overdrive. Baker & Taylor is a major distributor of print books and now reaches into the ebook world. There are some additional, smaller companies, most of those serving the academic world.

Authors don't upload directly to any of these companies; books are uploaded to one of the third-party aggregator sites. Note: Each of these companies is growing and adding new connections. This list *will* change during 2019.

Draft2Digital (D2D)

Overdrive, Baker & Taylor and Bibliotheca. The first two sell your book to a library for a fixed amount, and the library loans it to one person at a time, One Copy, One User (OCOU). Bibliotheca offers that and a program where you're paid a smaller amount every time the book is checked out, or Cost Per Checkout (CPC). A library may be willing to take a chance on a new author with the CPC system.

Kobo

Kobo's parent company Rakuten owns Overdrive, so you can upload directly here. Because Kobo is Overdrive, you earn a slightly higher royalty: 50% instead of 46.75% from D2D.

Smashwords

Overdrive, Baker & Taylor and Bibliotheca with just a single set-price purchase for unlimited checkouts, the OCOU system. Smashwords pays 45% of list price for sales with library aggregators.

PublishDrive

Overdrive and Bibliotheca.

StreetLib

Overdrive: They pay 40% of list price for wholesale (which a library purchase is).

While it at first seems bleak for indies and libraries, new doors are opening, and as indie books become more respected, those doors will open wider.

Bookstores

Then there's the dream of books sitting on bookstore shelves. We walk into the store and there they are. Before we leave, we turn one to the front so everyone can see the cover.

I'm sorry to wake you up from that lovely dream, but you probably won't see your books on many, if any, bookstore shelves. And you may not want to once you've learned more about it.

First, to understand the book industry, you need to realize that there are millions of book titles on Amazon. Millions. Now, picture a bookstore. Count the number of books on a shelf and multiply it. The store can't hold millions of books. It can only have a select few from the books that are released each year and some of the winners from previous years.

This is one of those times when a traditional publisher has ways into the situation that you don't. A trad book, especially one from one of the Big 5 publishers, could find space in a bookstore. But, and there's a big but, that may be for a short time. New releases have about six to eight weeks in a bookstore to prove that they're sellers and should be kept. Those which aren't are boxed up and returned. This is one of the reasons a traditional publisher pumps its money and effort into the book launch.

Bookstores are unique in the retail world because the books are on consignment. The store can return them if they want to, in any condition.

The steps to be considered by a bookstore are:

Reaching bookstores step 1:

Publish your print books with a company tied to a distributor bookstores buy from. Amazon is their major competitor, so if they can tell your book is printed by Amazon, they may or may not carry it. IngramSpark is owned by the massive distributor Ingram, one of the largest if not the largest book distributor in the world, so a company every bookstore should know.

Reaching bookstores step 2:

Set your discount rate to 55%. This percentage is the bookstore standard. They want to make a profit and the distributor takes a percentage too. Setting your percentage this high does shrink income from print book sales to libraries or readers because with IngramSpark, the only POD printer that allows you to adjust this, you could have set it as low as 30%.

Let's look an example of 55% vs. 30% (and you can set it anywhere in between.)

You plan to sell your print book for $14.95. We'll assume it's a 6" x 9" 200-page book. It costs $3.58 to print.

$14.95 minus 55% is $6.72 minus the print cost of $3.58 is $3.14.

$14.95 minus 30% is $10.47 minus the print cost of $3.58 is $6.89.

That's a big difference so your end goals would need to be part of this decision.

Reaching bookstores step 3:

Choose to allow returns in the US and Canada. Again, this is an Ingram-only decision to make. I was given this advice about the two countries by my former Ingram rep. Books *must* be set to returnable for bookstores because bookstores return books that don't sell. If you're at an event that sells your books, they'll also box up and return those that don't sell. You can choose to have the returned books destroyed by Ingram or delivered to you for a fee.

The decision to set up your book so it can sell to bookstores is individual and yours, but make sure that you have connections with bookstores before you choose the higher discount rate. You can change your mind later, and adjust the discount or returns.

I had thought that stores along the Alaska cruise path would be a good fit for my Alaska romances. I contacted them, set my discount to 55% and waited. Some did order books, but many are in tiny towns, and the volume wasn't enough to have the higher discount make sense. Potential income was lost with every other paperback sold through IngramSpark. Then a store returned some books at the end of the tourist season, as stores can do, and that cost me. I returned the discount to my normal, lower rate and moved on.

Local bookstores, just like your local library, may be happy to carry your books. The most prominent independent bookstore in my city required that I bring in a sample copy of my book for them to review. When they decided the kids' mysteries passed their inspection, they wanted to buy, but my discount rate wasn't what they needed, so they bought directly from me.

Can you get into libraries and bookstores? The answer is a solid . . . maybe. With some effort, the probability of that happening can climb higher.

Action Steps:

- **For libraries, decide if being in libraries is a major focus.**
- **Check the rules for review publications and submit your book if appropriate.**
- **Research juried book events you would be willing to travel to and enter your book into them.**

- Decide if your book has regional appeal and contact libraries in that area.
- Go wide with your ebooks and use an aggregator to reach libraries.
- Create a list of all libraries you want to reach and call them when your book is out in print and ebook, if wide.
- For bookstores, decide if a major focus will be getting your book on bookstore shelves.
- Set up your books on IngramSpark with returns and the discount rate at 55%.
- Create a plan for contacting bookstores through marketing.

TWENTY-EIGHT
SHOULD I TURN MY BOOK INTO AN AUDIOBOOK?

In this chapter: The ins and outs of making and distributing an audiobook

Audiobook sales are growing daily. It's obviously more complicated to create an audiobook than an ebook—you need a narrator in a studio, the audio needs to be edited, etc., so this wouldn't be your best first format with your first book. Get at least an ebook up for sale, then consider audio.

There are two main ways to pay for creating an audiobook:

Royalty share: The narrator works for free with the author agreeing to split the money earned from sales. This can only be done through ACX.

Pay up front: The author pays in full up front.

There's an occasional third version where the agreement is royalty share, but the narrator requires some money up front to pay for editing and other expenses.

Narrators are paid for the *finished hours* of the book. They've recorded more hours than the finished hours, editing as they go, but the author pays for the actual number of hours, the play time, of the completed audiobook. To estimate, use 9,000 words per finished hour. A 63,000-word book would be about seven hours long. Of course, writing style and the narrator will make this vary. A suspenseful book may read faster than a business book.

You have quite a few options for both creating and selling your audiobook.

ACX

ACX, an Amazon company, distributes through multiple channels, one of which is Audible, also an Amazon company. ACX is the home of royalty split audiobook production. ACX can also be your source for narration you pay for.

On ACX, the author sets up a profile, chooses a page or two they'd like read for an audition, reviews narrators (what they call "producers"), can ask for samples, chooses one narrator and begins the process. Narrators vary in skill level and the quality of the equipment they're using. It's up to the author to choose wisely. Ask friends and/or family, especially those who enjoy audiobooks in your genre, to listen to the samples with you. You, the author, have final say, but input could be helpful.

If you're paying up front, you have the option of non-exclusive or exclusive distribution, meaning only available through ACX and the partners they choose or available wherever you choose.

Non-exclusive: Royalty 25%

Exclusive: Royalty 40% if the author pays upfront for the recording. If it's a royalty split, it's 20% each to the author and the producer. A bonus for those choosing to be exclusive is that once a title is live, you can request 25 promo codes, specifying US or UK, and give away the Audible version of the book to reviewers and other influencers.

If the author paid up front and chose exclusive, she can change from exclusive to non-exclusive after one year.

Either way: *Audible will have the right to distribute your audiobook for seven years (R).* But with non-exclusive, you can also use your choice of additional distributors.

Prices are not set by the author; the various retailers set the price.

A benefit of ACX and Audible is that you can refer people to the Audible store in the US, UK, France, or Germany, and if they're a new member and purchase their first audiobook, you'll earn a $75 bounty. This applies to exclusive and non-exclusive. If you used royalty share, you'll receive $50 and your royalty collaborator will receive $25.

Payment is monthly.

If you're happy with those terms, great. If you're interested in exploring other options, those exist. If you choose to be non-exclusive, then you can make arrangements to distribute your book through other channels.

Other audiobook production options

Another choice is to simply find a narrator on your own and contract the work. Or you could hire another company which offers narrators and distribution. Two of those are Findaway Voices and ListenUp Audiobooks.

Findaway Voices:

This may be the most prominent audiobook company right now after ACX. Their distribution grew during 2018, in part due to the addition of Storytel. The website says their distribution network reaches "nearly every country in the world." Findaway Voices is the narration arm of Findaway, a distributor.

Many authors learned of Findaway Voices when Draft2Digital partnered with them in 2017 and Smashwords in 2018. Going through D2D takes away the normal $49 admin fee.

The author pays up front for narration; there isn't a royalty split option.

The people at Findaway Voices review your book and recommend narrators, who have been vetted for quality. You can request a sample and give them a section you'd like read. Choose one that would show you their skills for your book—funny, dramatic, suspenseful, quirky—whatever will help you see that narrator's skills applied to your writing style. If you love it, the first fifteen minutes is recorded. Once approved, you'll receive completed chapters for review and feedback.

Audiobooks are quality checked before going live.

The audiobook would still be on Amazon and Audible, but with a non-exclusive agreement and no long-term rights agreement. You own the rights.

The author also sets the price and chooses which stores to sell through. The royalty rate with audiobook vendors varies from about 25% to 50%. Findaway Voices takes a 20% commission from your royalties.

Payment is monthly.

Giveaway codes: For every title, authors receive 30 Authors Direct Giveaway Codes that you can give to potential reviewers and influencers.

ListenUp Audiobooks:

This company also does narration and distribution.

Kobo partnered with them in 2018. Using Kobo for your ListenUp book gives you a $100 discount per finished audiobook hour.

Once ListenUp understands your project, they'll offer several audio samples to consider. Once you've approved your narrator, they'll send you a production contract and schedule.

You can work with ListenUp to create an audiobook, but don't have to distribute with them. They distribute through many channels including Findaway.

The audiobook would still be on Amazon and Audible, but with a non-exclusive agreement and no long-term rights agreement. You own the rights.

Through Kobo, they pay 75% of the royalty the

vendor pays—that's a 25% commission. Audiobooks purchased on the ListenUp website earn the full 75% of list price.

Going directly through ListenUp (not through Kobo), the split is 80% royalties paid, 20% commission. Then the books sold on their website receive 80% of list price. Of course, you wouldn't have had the discount and it may take a while to earn that amount.

Payment is quarterly.

Distributor Options

Each of these companies produced and distributed audiobooks. If you have a nonexclusive agreement with ACX or produce your audiobook elsewhere, you could use a distributor such as Authors Republic.

Audiobook Covers

These are different than every other book format. They're perfectly square, not rectangular. ACX's specs suit most of the industry, with one addition. Your cover designer is probably familiar with audiobooks, but it's always a good idea to clearly state what you need.

ACX says:

No smaller than 2400 x 2400 pixels.

24-bit (True Color) minimum.

No smaller than 72 dpi resolution.

RGB color (not CYMK).

Images must be a true square, not a rectangular image with borders.

JPG, PNG, and TIF file formats only.

Include author name and title.

I asked Findaway Voices if these specs worked for

all vendors and was told to up the resolution to 3000 x 3000 pixels for a great look on services like Apple Books.

If you're wondering, as I did, if I could take my regular book cover, put it on a square box and add colored bands on the sides to fill in the blank area, I learned that when colored bars are added, it's known as shadowboxing and some vendors including Amazon's Audible will not accept those covers. Some vendors would, but you wouldn't want to lose the Amazon audiobook sales.

Action Steps:

- **Decide if and when you would like to have your book made into an audiobook.**
- **If you're ready now, decide about paying up front or doing a royalty split.**
- **If paying up front, decide which company you want to use.**

TWENTY-NINE

DO I WANT A LARGE PRINT OR HARDCOVER VERSION OF MY BOOK?

In this chapter: If having your book in large print or hardcover would be helpful

Large Print

Large print may be worth considering. The majority but not all of your large print readers will be senior citizens, so this would best suit books read by people that age. A book for kids or about makeup techniques may not be a best seller in large print.

There's the belief that anyone who needs larger print can simply read an ebook with its super adjustable type size. Not all of the readers who need larger text are tech savvy.

My romances are all in large print. I made them as hardcover large print. If I did it again, I would make them as large print paperback so they could be priced at the less expensive paperback price.

If you format print yourself, it's easy to format large print. If not, ask your paperback formatter for a quote.

The real cost is usually in the revised cover for the thicker book with its wider spine.

Hardcover or Hardback Books

Some books may release as hardcover. A special holiday edition or a journal could work well that way. This is the exception, not the rule.

My children's mysteries are all in hardcover. Some libraries didn't want to buy them unless they were in hardcover. I've also sold some off Amazon, I'm assuming to parents or grandparents who preferred hardcover over paperback. Unless your book is best in hardcover, the decision to add this format to your offerings is one best left until everything else is under control.

Action Steps:

- **Decide if you're going to start with large print or hardcover books.**
- **If not now, do you want to add them in the future?**

THIRTY
SHOULD I TO PAY TO COPYRIGHT MY BOOK?

In this chapter: Learn about copyrighting your book

In the United States, the creator of a work automatically owns the copyright to it. It belongs to you when you create it.

Use the copyright symbol on your copyright page:

© 2019 Shannon L. Brown.

With that said, according to an attorney I spoke with, officially having it copyrighted is useful if you're ever in a situation with plagiarism or something similar.*

If you do decide to register your book, the directions are clear on the site (R). The cost of filing online for a single title using the Single Application filing system is $35. The office prefers that you upload a digital copy of the book if you're using this system. Paper filing costs more.

You can upload an ebook when using the online system. All applicants are required to send the "Best

Edition" of their book within three months of publication.

Outside the US:

Please check your country's rules. New regulations in the EU will be changing online copyright rules there and perhaps elsewhere which may effect book copyrighting. It's easy to check the rules.

*Remember: I'm not an attorney. You're responsible for the decisions you make and the legal ramifications of them. (Sorry about another warning.)

Action Step:

- **Decide if you're going to officially copyright your book.**

THIRTY-ONE

THIS WHOLE INDIE THING SEEMS STRESSFUL!

In this chapter: How to be a calm self-publisher

Take a deep breath. If you're publishing books for fun, keep it fun. If you want to make writing books and indie publishing your full-time work, you'll need to stay calm and keep moving on. And I don't mean to sound flippant. Staying calm is one of the keys to succeeding long-term.

It's easy to be pulled in ten or twenty directions at any time. You're writing, no you're editing, no you're formatting, no you're marketing. Oh, did I remember to send out my newsletter? I forgot??? But I have to edit my book now.

Take a deep breath. Being an indie author isn't just a short-term goal, it's finding a way to do the work while being healthy physically and emotionally.

I pushed myself in ways that weren't healthy, always scrambling to get everything done. I burned out and didn't write fiction for a whole year. Fortunately, I can write nonfiction almost anytime because I was a journalist before I was a published author, and I'm used to writing to pay the bills.

I've learned to do one thing at a time. That sounds like a simple concept, but it isn't. When you're writing, write. When you're marketing, only do that. You can do multiple activities in a day, allowing blocks of time for each, or you can set aside entire days for each. The problem comes when you're trying to do many things at the same time. You need a website and a newsletter and . . .

Choose one thing, do it well, then move on to the next thing. It may seem like you're getting nowhere if you're only working on your newsletter for a day, but you'll go further faster if you get it done right the first time.

Complete the task, or the portion of it you're working on in that time block, before going to the next thing.

And keep focused on the final goal of publishing books. The market will continue to change, but you'll remain steady and steadfast through it.

Action Steps:

- **Relax.**
- **Take publishing your book one step at a time.**

AFTERWORD

I hope Self-Publishing Secrets helped you learn how to publish your book. Don't forget to go the the Resources page to find up-to-date links. As I learn about new tools, tips, and other info, I'll add them to the page. Go to shannonbrown.co/resources.

NOTES:

Made in the USA
Middletown, DE
19 February 2019